BALADI

PALESTINE – *A CELEBRATION OF FOOD FROM LAND AND SEA*

JOUDIE KALLA

FOOD PHOTOGRAPHY
BY JAMIE ORLANDO SMITH

First published in 2018

A Jacqui Small book for White Lion Publishing,
part of the Quarto Group

The Old Brewery, 6 Blundell Street
London N7 9BH, United Kingdom
T (0)20 7700 6700 F (0)20 7700 8066
www.QuartoKnows.com

Publisher: Jacqui Small
Managing Editor: Abi Waters
Design and Art Direction: Rachel Cross
Commissioning Editor: Fritha Saunders
Editor: Rachel Malig
Photographer: Jamie Orlando Smith
Production: Maeve Healy

Extract from 'On This Earth' by Mahmoud Darwish
(page 11) reproduced with kind permission of the
Mahmoud Darwish Foundation

The author has made every attempt to draw attention to
safety precautions, but it is the reader's responsibility to
ensure safety practices while carrying out techniques
outlined in this book.

ISBN: 978-1-911127-86-4

A catalogue record for this book is available
from the British Library.

2020 2019 2018
10 9 8 7 6 5 4 3 2 1

Printed in China

BALADI

CONTENTS

Previous page: Misilyah Village, Jenin
Left: Areeha (Jericho)

Introduction

I love the word 'Baladi'. As with most Arabic words, it has many meanings, but above all it means 'my home, my land, my country'. To me, Palestine is all of these things, and not just in a geographical sense, but in the sense of my life and my family, too. It has been home for my family for hundreds of years, and embodies everything I am and everything I have been raised to be. I feel very blessed to have been born a Palestinian, and to have a platform to discuss all the wonderful things about this amazing, deep-rooted, historical, religious and cultural country with so much to offer – especially in the culinary department.

While talking about Palestine, one must understand the deep complexities that run through this piece of land. Over time it has been in the hands of many, which has resulted in a huge influx of different cultures. Palestinians have struggled to retain their identity through this occupation for over 70 years, and as a people it has made us louder and more focused on keeping our history and our traditions well and truly alive, passed on to future generations through music, design, food, technology, art and literature.

As with many Palestinians, almost 700,000 to be precise, my family were among those who had to flee their homes in 1948 during the Nakba (the catastrophe that resulted in their expulsion), and with that came major changes, such as having to start life in a new place, and adapt to a different way of living and eating. Although the countries surrounding Palestine may seem similar, in fact they are very different. It is as you would find in Europe – countries may be close to one another, but the traditions and lifestyle are not the same. My grandparents had to adjust, and over time their food changed, mixing with Jordanian, Lebanese, Egyptian, and most importantly Syrian food.

The Palestine of my grandparents was known for its abundance of fresh fruit, vegetables and herbs. It is true that there are areas of luscious greenery, with fruit, citrus, almond and olive trees scattered across the landscape. Yet throughout the different regions, you will find different terrains – areas of uninhabited land that looks like desert, and colder areas such as Safad in the north near the Lebanese border. In some you have more grains and pulses, while others are more fruit and vegetable based. And then you have the beautiful sea routes, near Yaffa, Gaza and Haifa, which carry a different cuisine to the rest of the country, that is fresh, tangy, herby and spicy, heavily laden with fish and vegetables. Today, all over the country, life continues in the ground, above the ground and all around you in defiance of the daily hardships of life under occupation. This is the fabric of Palestine and its people. When you are situated in such a place on the earth, with all seasons and a cross trade from Europe through to Asia, you cannot help but create the most wonderful dishes from all the produce at your fingertips.

This book was very exciting to write, because I had the chance to look at Palestine anew, step by step, through different areas, different seasons, and cuisines that change from location to location. Looking at how certain towns and cities cook the same dishes so differently that they are almost unrecognizable has really opened my eyes to the fact that even internally the country has its own differences from region to region. I have made choices as to which versions to include here based on the way my own family cooks them, but that is not to say other ways are not correct.

Opposite, clockwise from top left: Ramallah; Gaza Seaport; Old City, Al-Nasira (Nazareth); Al-Khalil (Hebron)

Some may question the origins of these recipes, and whether they are truly Palestinian. My grandparents lived in Palestine until they were in their mid-thirties, so the basis of their food culture was purely Palestinian until then. This is how we eat in our home, how I cooked at my restaurant and now cook at events. It is what I learnt from my mother and her mother. The majority of recipes are authentically Palestinian, but I also try to bring a little of other countries to your table too, reflecting my family's real life experience in every way. It is the essence of Baladi – home – wherever that may be. I think it is important to know that you can create many dishes that have a nostalgic feel to them without recreating a specific dish from a specific place. We are made up of the fabric of so many experiences, and this is what I love about our food.

It is also important to note that everyone has a different experience and lifestyle, as we do in other parts of the world, and adaptations to recipes and styles vary according to personal taste. We are a heavily garlic, chilli and lemon obsessed family, as you will soon find out. But this is just the way we like things. You can by all means add and change things to your own preference – more spicy, more salty, less tart, everything is possible.

We also like to experiment with our ingredients too, as you will see with desserts such as the Chocolate and Labneh Cake (page 234) and Knafeh Cheesecake (page 224), and some raw fish dishes like the Sea Bream Ceviche (page 182). This is where I introduce recipes that I am familiar with, and make them my own, always with the essence of home. For me, everything is traced back to Palestine, as it is what I am most familiar with. Even after working in kitchens for ten years, cooking different cuisines, it never changed the core of who I am. So trying new things with old traditions is always good.

When I talk to my mother about recipes, we start discussing a recipe in depth, then in a flash she starts talking about another, and another, that all spin off from the first. The number of recipes stored in her head is simply unbelievable. She sometimes has to stop for a second as she realizes firstly that I can't write that fast, and also that I have perhaps never heard of a certain dish before. The most amazing thing about working with her so closely is that it has brought back so many of her own forgotten memories, and has really ignited something in her to cook more than she already does. The bond between cooking and memories, creating flashbacks to another time, is something that I am so pleased to have been a part of with her and my twenty aunties, who are all so excited to be resurrecting recipes that they too had forgotten. I am delighted to be able to share them with you, for you to hopefully cook and experience as well.

Some dishes may seem familiar to people who have never eaten Palestinian food before, because we have such a multi-faceted trade route that crosses so many borders. There will be dishes such as *Shishbarak* (page 105) which are familiar to people from Russia and the Ukraine, and others which are eaten from Spain to Italy and Eastern Europe, perhaps just made with different spices. We have a common thread that weaves through us, which makes us all family in the end.

This book has been a labour of love, and I could not have showcased the beauty of Palestine without all the amazing photographers who live in every corner, and who have created a journey for all of us to walk through, allowing us to feel a part of it, to lose ourselves in this land and its people. Living in the diaspora, we have different experiences to those who live in Palestine, but our history is ingrained in all of us, no matter where we live. It's our roots that are important – like the glorious olive tree, which is our symbol of hope, history and connection to our land.

One of the most important things for me in writing this book was that it was educational and inspiring, showing how so many beautiful and wonderful things can come out of such a complex country, and highlighting some amazing dishes that are not often eaten any more. Most importantly, it is about the idea of community and family, conversations and stories that I hope to be able to tell for a long time to my own family, and for others to share with theirs.

One of my favourite poets, Mahmoud Darwish, is a beacon for Palestine and all her glory, writing literally thousands of poems about our country. The love story behind his words, the several meanings that come from a single word, describe her in ways that can only make you want to know her more. My favourite poem is called 'We have on this earth what makes life worth living', and I couldn't agree more.

Joudie Kalla

We have on this earth what makes life
  worth living,
On this land there is that which deserves life:
On this earth, there is the lady of the land,
The Mother of beginnings, the Mother of endings.
She was called Palestine, Her name later
  became Palestine.
My lady, because you are my lady, I have
  all of that which makes life worth living.
  I deserve life.

MAHMOUD DARWISH
(1941–2008)

Opposite, clockwise from top left: *Beit Lahem (Bethlehem); Akka;*
Nablus; **This page:** *Gaza; Al-Khalil (Hebron); Al-Auja, Areeha (Jericho)*

Markets and Village Life

VEGETABLES, CHEESES, PRESERVES AND DRINKS

Market life is part of the traditional culture of Palestine and still very much alive today. The market forms the hub of each town, with vendors selling sweets, breads, olives, dried spices, herbs, and even breakfast dishes such as *Qudsiyeh* (page 37), *Ful Bil Bayd* (page 36) and *Shakshoukeh* (page 30). My grandparents would not do a weekly shop, as we are now accustomed to, but would buy whatever was fresh from the sellers each day, enjoying the shop while having a cup of Arabic coffee (page 21) or some *Dibs Wa Tahineh* (page 20) and catching up with friends, who were also picking up their daily bread, and dinner for the night. Although my grandparents were from different parts of Palestine – my father's family were from Safad in the north, which was known for its mills and bakeries; my mother's family were from El-Lydd and Yaffa in the more central coastal area, where textiles, fine pottery and dyes were famous – the market traditions were the same. Only the food differed, according to what was available on their land at any given time of the season.

Market culture has changed little with time: when freedom of movement is not restricted, the markets are bustling with locals, and with the tourists visiting this holy land. What could be better than walking down the street and seeing people enjoying what their country has to offer, such as pickled *Makdous* (page 48) and *Feta Bil Zayt* (page 49) in peppery green olive oil from trees that are thousands of years old. We lose this in more western parts of the world, where farmers' markets appear once a week. Imagine the same market, every day, all year round – this is the pulse running through Palestine, keeping life as natural and original as possible. The market is the place to begin your day in Palestine, and in this chapter you will see why.

This page: Jenin
Overleaf (left) top: Old City, Al-Quds (Jerusalem); bottom: Beit Lahem (Bethlehem); (right): Old City, Al-Quds

From left to right: Dibs wa tahineh; Haleeb wa curcuma bil hail; Qahweh Arabiyeh

Dibs wa tahineh

دبس وطحينة

Grape molasses and tahini

Ok, so this isn't really a recipe, but I just couldn't leave it out on the basis that it only has two ingredients. This is the Palestinian equivalent of peanut butter and jam: a bowl of tahini with some grape molasses drizzled over. It is best eaten on toasted bread or dipped into as a sweet treat. I love this and really think it is under-rated. Perhaps many people don't write about it because it is so simple . . . You should try it with a hot cup of Arabic coffee – it will get your morning off to a fabulous start!

Serves 2

100ml tahini
large drizzle of grape
  molasses
toasted bread, to serve

Place the tahini in a bowl and drizzle over the grape molasses. Scoop onto toasted bread and enjoy.

Haleeb wa curcuma bil hail

حليب وكركم بالهال

Turmeric milk with cracked cardamom pods

We use turmeric sparingly in our food, but it does appear, most importantly in our drinks. We make this drink all the time – the infusion of the cardamom pods really elevates it and makes it so soothing. I don't know about you, but any dish with cardamom, especially if it is warm, just makes everything better. We also use cardamom in our Arabic coffee, which is simply divine. The aroma just wafts through the house, creating the feel of a festive season all year round. We all know that turmeric has so many good properties; not only does it help with inflammation but also with digestion, and drinking this after a meal is always soothing.

Serves 4

700ml full-fat milk
3–4 tsp ground turmeric
  (depends on how strong
  you like it)
5–6 cracked cardamom
  pods
pinch of cracked black
  pepper
1 tsp ground ginger
1 tbsp honey

Place all the ingredients in a pan over a low heat, stir to combine, then let it simmer until all the flavours are infused. Keep whisking as the mixture heats, as the turmeric tends to fall to the bottom of the pan.

Once the ingredients are combined and you are happy with the flavour, pour into four cups and serve.

Above: Gaza

Qahweh Arabiyeh

قهوة عربية

Arabic coffee

Arabic coffee runs in the veins of most Palestinians. It is thick, scented and smooth, but it has a real kick of caffeine. There are so many versions and variations throughout the Middle East and the Gulf that you could dedicate a whole chapter to it, but we like it simple. With a hint of cardamom. We use coffee with cardamom already in it, but if you can't find this, you can add your own; as a guide, I use 2 teaspoons per 500g of coffee. This is typically made with espresso-style cups.

Serves 2

1 heaped tsp Arabic coffee per person

2 espresso-style coffee cups of water per every tsp of coffee used

sugar, to taste

pinch of ground cardamom

Place the coffee in a pot and cover with water – if you use 2 teaspoons of coffee, add 4 cups of water (measure out using your coffee cups), and so on. Add sugar to taste, and the cardamom (if it isn't already in the coffee), and bring to the boil.

Let it bubble to the top, remove it from the heat for a second, then return it and let it bubble again; repeat this two or three times, just to make sure the coffee has brewed properly. Then let it sit for a moment so the coffee grains don't come to the top but form a dense layer at the bottom. Serve and enjoy.

Mshaat m'a dagga

مشاط مع دقة

Cauliflower fritters with a spicy tomato sauce

My favourite way of eating eggs is to add some kind of vegetable, lots of herbs, spices, chilli, garlic and some form of salsa on top. In my first book, *Palestine on a Plate*, I included a dish called *Ijeh* – a slightly fluffy fritter, like a pancake, with lots of herbs and spices in it. This is a similar recipe, but made with cauliflower florets. I have included it in this book because it's something that we eat all the time as Palestinians and it couldn't be missed. Some people make them more dough-like, but I prefer them to be eggy and omelette-like. You can experiment to see which you prefer.

Serves 4

½ head of cauliflower, cut into florets

1 heaped tsp ground turmeric

100g fresh flat-leaf parsley, chopped

1 onion, finely diced

2 garlic cloves, crushed

1 green chilli, diced

½ tsp caraway powder

6 eggs

¼ tsp baking powder

2 tsp plain flour

olive oil

salt and freshly ground black pepper

1 x quantity Spicy Tomato Sauce (page 156), to serve

Khubez (page 89), to serve

Place the cauliflower florets into a pan of boiling water with the turmeric and 1 teaspoon of salt, and cook for about 4 minutes to add both colour and flavour. They should be soft but not mushy, so allow a minute or two longer if necessary.

Once they are done, transfer the florets onto kitchen towel to drain, and set aside to cool.

Combine the parsley, onion, garlic, chilli, caraway, eggs, baking powder and flour together in a bowl.

Once the florets are cool, gently flatten them in your hand. Heat a little oil in a small frying pan. Place one cauliflower floret into the pan and ladle a serving of the egg mixture on top to form a circle. Cook for about 30 seconds, then flip it over when it has slightly browned and cook on the other side; the whole process should take a maximum of 1–2 minutes.

Remove from the oil, set aside, and repeat with the remaining cauliflower and egg mixture.

You can eat them on their own, but my mum loves putting them into little pita pockets and drizzling the spicy *dagga* sauce all over them.

Halloumi mashwi ma' bayd

حلومة مشوية مع بيض

Grilled halloumi, fried eggs and roasted tomatoes

Halloumi cheese is used a lot in Palestinian cooking. Other cheeses such as Akkawi, feta and Nabulsi are also used, and are staples of the Palestinian kitchen, but the best cheese for grilling is halloumi. When I'm hungry and want something quick to eat with full flavour, this is what I make. It's quick, easy and delicious. The roasting of the tomatoes always reminds me of my dad and the famous barbecues that we used to have.

Serves 2

2 tbsp olive oil

1 plum tomato, halved

1 x 225g packet of halloumi
   cheese, sliced

2 eggs

1 tsp za'atar

salt and freshly ground
   black pepper

Put the olive oil into a hot pan with the halved tomatoes, and season with a little salt and pepper. When they become slightly soft, tender and charred, add the halloumi cheese. It will start to brown slightly, like a tiger skin print, but don't move it around because you don't want it to secrete too much water.

While the halloumi and tomatoes are cooking, crack the eggs into the same pan, and season with salt, pepper and a sprinkling of za'atar. Cover with a lid just to cook the egg yolks slightly.

Transfer to a plate (or serve in the pan) and eat straight away, with plenty of radishes, cucumber and green chillies to accompany it.

Above: Jenin market

Labneh bil toum wa bayd

لبنة بالثوم وبيض

Garlic labneh, shatta and poached egg on taboon bread

We eat labneh almost every day – it's like the Middle Eastern version of probiotic yogurt – and so we like to change it up a little bit, mixing it with different breakfast dishes and actually making it the star of the show. The contrast of the tangy labneh against the creamy egg and spicy shatta is incredible.

Serves 2

200g fresh labneh
1 garlic clove, grated
2 *Khubez Taboon* (page 88)
2 tsp red Shatta (page 42)
2 (very fresh) eggs
1 tbsp white wine vinegar
 (optional)
1 tsp sumac
small bunch of fresh dill
salt and cracked black
 pepper

Mix the labneh and grated garlic in a bowl. If you can't find labneh, you can use very thick Greek yogurt.

Place your taboon breads on a plate and slather the garlic labneh on top. Drizzle 1 teaspoon of the red shatta over each bread.

To poach the eggs, bring a pan of water to a simmer and season it with salt. I also add white wine vinegar to my water, as it helps to bind the egg. Place 1 egg at a time into the water and create a swirling motion so the white begins to wrap around the yolk. Cook it for 2–3 minutes, then remove it from the water with a slotted spoon, place on one of the taboon breads and repeat with the other egg.

Season with salt and pepper, scatter over a little sumac and dill and serve.

Above: Jenin

Bayd ma' batata

بيض مع بطاطا

Pan-fried potatoes with herbs, spices and smashed eggs

Serves 2

1 large potato, peeled and
  cut into small cubes
4 tbsp olive oil
1 banana shallot, diced
1 garlic clove, smashed
sprinkle of paprika
sprinkle of cayenne pepper
4 eggs
fresh coriander, chopped
Khubez (page 89), to serve
salt and freshly ground
  black pepper

This whole chapter reminds me of my dad. All the recipes are dishes he was not only good at making, but also loved to eat – the staples that appeared on his table as he was growing up in Safad in the north of Palestine.

Parboil the potatoes in a pan of boiling water for 5–7 minutes, then drain.

Place the oil, parboiled potatoes, shallots and garlic into a frying pan and sauté for a while until the potatoes are soft. Once the potatoes and shallots have softened, add the spices and mix to combine.

Separate the potatoes in the pan into four equal portions and crack an egg on top of each. Move the mixture around over a low heat and stir together. I don't like to overscramble the eggs as I like to have bigger chunks of yolk present.

Season to taste, then add the coriander and serve warm with some *khubez*.

Salatet tahineh

سلطة طحينة

Mixed vegetable salad with tahini dressing

Serves 2–4

5 radishes, cubed
1 cucumber, cubed
2 plum tomatoes, cubed
crunchy head of gem
  lettuce, roughly chopped
small bunch of fresh
  flat-leaf parsley, chopped
juice of 2 lemons
2 tbsp tahini
2 tbsp Greek yogurt
olive oil, to drizzle
salt

This salad is typical in all parts of Palestine. We serve it with falafels, and as a side to fish dishes and meat. It can also be eaten on its own. It is fresh and crunchy with a kick of lemon and tahini.

Make sure all the vegetables are cubed to the same size, then set aside in a bowl with the parsley.

Combine the lemon juice, tahini, yogurt and a little salt in a large bowl. Check for seasoning and add some more tahini or yogurt if you prefer. This should be a thick but droppable consistency. Add the mixed vegetables and stir to combine, drizzle with a little olive oil, and serve.

Shakshoukeh khadra

شكشوكة خضرة

Green shakshoukeh

Shakshoukeh is one of the most recognizable dishes in the Levant, possibly originating in North Africa. The word itself means 'a mixture', or to mix and combine, which exactly describes how all the ingredients work so well together to form a beautiful dish, that is so much more than eggs and sauce. My Teta Najla was famous for hers, using green tomatoes in place of the more traditional red tomatoes, and this recipe is quite simply divine. The smoky cumin and paprika really bring out the flavours. My Teta lived by the sea and used lots of green leaves, herbs and vegetables in her version, reflecting the freshness of the produce in her local area.

Serves 4

3 tbsp olive oil

1 large leek, sliced into rings

2 garlic cloves, finely chopped

1 green pepper, diced

1 green chilli, chopped

1 red chilli, chopped

6 large green tomatoes, cut into rings

500ml water

bunch of Swiss chard, stalks removed, cut into bite-sized pieces

20g fresh oregano leaves

1 tsp ground cumin

1 tsp paprika

4 large eggs

salt and freshly ground black pepper

Khubez Taboon (page 88), to serve

Preheat the oven to 190ºC Fan (210ºC/415ºF/Gas 6–7).

Place the olive oil into an ovenproof pan over a medium–low heat and add the leeks. Slowly cook them down for 3–4 minutes until soft and tender. Add the garlic and green peppers and continue to cook for 5–6 minutes until softened.

Add the chillies and tomatoes and let them cook down for 6–7 minutes to create a thick sauce. Add the water and cook for 7–8 minutes, then add the chard and allow it to wilt into the mix.

Once the flavours are all combined, add the fresh oregano leaves and season with salt and pepper. Add the spices, check again for seasoning, and once you are happy with the consistency and flavour, make four tiny wells in the thick sauce. Crack the eggs into them and place into the oven to bake for about 7 minutes, depending on how well you like your eggs cooked.

Serve with some *khubez taboon* and eat immediately.

Baba's soft-boiled eggs with yogurt, chilli and lemon

بيض برشت مع لبن و فلفل احمر وليمون

Ever since I can remember, my dad would eat his eggs like this. I never understood how he could put lemon on eggs, but my dad will put lemon on everything – and chilli, and garlic. And the result of this is that now we all do the same. These eggs are so delicious – I adore the creaminess of the yogurt mixed with the super-soft eggs and drizzled with olive oil and chilli. It is so good, and then you get this little kick of lemon, which balances out the creaminess of it all.

Serves 2

4 eggs
1–2 tbsp thick Greek yogurt
juice of 1 lemon
pinch of chilli flakes
olive oil, to drizzle
fresh parsley, chopped
salt and freshly ground
   black pepper

Bring a pan of water to the boil and boil the eggs for 5 minutes. You can cook them for longer if you prefer – we just like them soft-textured.

Once the eggs have cooked, peel them and break them into a plate or bowl. Add the yogurt, lemon juice, chilli flakes and a little salt and pepper, and check for seasoning. Personally I prefer mine to have extra chilli, but it's good to start with a small pinch.

Drizzle with olive oil, sprinkle over some fresh parsley and devour it quickly!

Above: East Al-Quds (Jerusalem)

From left to right: Ful bil bayd; Qudsiyeh

Ful bil bayd

فول بالبيض

Smashed broad beans, tomato and fresh green chilli with fried eggs

Smashed broad beans and eggs are two of my favourite things. I love having something spicy, tangy and garlicky for breakfast, and the combination of these two together is so delicious, you'll wonder why you haven't had it before. I don't tend to smash the broad beans too much; I like to keep some chunks so you can actually feel the texture against the eggs. They have a very similar smooth consistency, and they work perfectly well with the fresh green chilli and lemon.

Serves 2–4

2 x 400g tins of brown
  broad beans
2 garlic cloves, chopped
juice of 1 lemon
1 green chilli, chopped
1 tomato, diced
olive oil
4 eggs
bunch of fresh flat-leaf
  parsley, chopped
salt and freshly ground
  black pepper

Put the tinned broad beans into a pan with their liquid. Add the garlic, lemon juice, chillies, tomatoes and a splash of olive oil, and place over a low heat. You don't want it to bubble, just simmer gently for about 5 minutes.

Heat a little olive oil in another pan, then crack the eggs into the pan and gently fry them until cooked through and the yolk is still slightly runny. Add salt and pepper to taste.

Transfer the beans to a serving dish and top with the fried eggs. Sprinkle with some chopped parsley and serve with the bread of your choice.

Right: Jenin

Above: *Dome of the Rock, Old City, Al-Quds (Jerusalem)*

Qudsiyeh

قدسية

Hummus and broad bean purée with olive oil and parsley

Serves 4

2 x 400g tins of brown
   broad beans
2 garlic cloves, chopped
juice of 1 lemon
1 green chilli, chopped
1 tomato, diced, plus a little
   extra to serve
1 tsp ground cumin
olive oil
fresh flat-leaf parsley,
   chopped, to serve

For the hummus

1 x 400g tin of chickpeas,
   drained
juice of 2 lemons
1 garlic clove, crushed
2 tbsp tahini
1 tbsp Greek yogurt
1–2 tsp salt

Qudsiyeh literally means Jerusalemite, which indicates that this dish originated in Al-Quds (Jerusalem). But it is eaten all over Palestine, in places like Akka, Al-Khalil (Hebron) and Yaffa. It is cheap and easy to make, and very nutritious, which is why it is so popular. I can't get enough of it, and always have plenty of chickpeas lying around my storecupboard. If you have time and want to make this from scratch, use dried beans and soak them overnight with a tablespoon of bicarbonate of soda, then boil them the next day for about 30–40 minutes before following the recipe below.

Put the tinned broad beans into a pan with their liquid. Add the garlic, lemon juice, chillies, tomatoes, cumin and a splash of olive oil, and place over a low heat. You don't want it to bubble, just simmer gently for about 5 minutes. Remove from the heat and purée the mixture using a food processor or stick blender.

Set aside a few whole chickpeas to serve, then place all the ingredients for the hummus in a blender or food processor and blend to a smooth paste.

Plate up the dish with the broad bean purée on the bottom, then top with the hummus. Drizzle with plenty of olive oil, and scatter over a few chopped tomatoes, the reserved chickpeas and fresh parsley. I always eat mine with warm toasted bread. Simply Palestine.

Betinjan makli bil a'sal wa tahineh

باذنجان مقلي بالعسل والطحينة

Fried aubergine slices with honey and tahini

My mother used to eat this during the days of Ramadan, in between breaking her fast and the following morning; this time of day is called *suhoor*. This dish is very simple to make, delicious and filling, with both a salty and sweet taste – always a good thing. You could serve this with bread or simply on its own. It is reminiscent of those long nights when you crave something hot, sweet and satisfying; and it's always good to have something nutritious with honey and tahini to start your day.

Serves 2

vegetable oil, for frying
1 aubergine, partially
   peeled lengthways to
   create stripes, then cut
   into 1cm-thick rings
2 tbsp tahini
a squeeze of honey
sea salt flakes

Place a little vegetable oil into a small pan over a medium heat; the hotter the oil the better, as you don't want the aubergines to be drenched in oil, you want them to fry. Cook the aubergines for a few minutes on both sides until a golden colour, then remove from the heat and transfer the slices to a serving dish.

Drizzle the tahini over the aubergine slices, followed by a little honey over the tahini, then add a sprinkle of sea salt flakes to balance out the sweetness.

Right: Jenin

*From left to right: Halloumi makliyeh
wa shatta; Shatta khadra wa hamra;
Hummus bil shatta*

Shatta khadra wa hamra

شطة خضرة وحمرة

Green and red shatta

Shatta is a traditional paste made from red or green chillies, garlic, vinegar and oil. It is found all over Palestine, but is most famous in the coastal areas of Gaza and Yaffa, where it is eaten on everything.

You will need

1 sterilized 750ml jar

500g red or green chillies
1 tsp apple cider vinegar
1–2 tsp salt
1 garlic clove, crushed
1 tsp golden caster sugar
small bunch of fresh flat-
  leaf parsley
olive oil

Remove the stalks from the chillies, keeping the seeds. I like to crush the chillies in a pestle and mortar (as my Teta used to do), or you can pulse them in a blender. You don't want them to be smashed to a complete paste – they should be rustic and chunky with some smooth bits.

Transfer the chillies to a bowl, add all the other ingredients except the olive oil, and mix together until you have a thick rustic paste. Taste for flavour: you may want to add more or less of something as everyone has an individual preference, but in general the paste should be spicy and used sparingly. Once you have finished, transfer to a jar and add the olive oil to cover the paste completely. The paste will keep in the fridge for several weeks once it is covered with the oil.

Halloumi makliyeh wa shatta

حلومة مقلية وشطة

Halloumi fries with tangy shatta

A more gluttonous version of grilled halloumi. I like to change recipes to make them my own, and here I'm serving a traditional chilli shatta with fried halloumi. The vinegar, sugar, salt and chilli create an amazing sensation in your mouth – this works a treat against the creamy, squeaky halloumi!

Serves 2–4

1 x 225g packet of halloumi
  cheese
2 egg yolks
plain flour
150g breadcrumbs (I use
  panko breadcrumbs)
sunflower oil, for frying
1 x quantity green or red
  Shatta (see above)

Cut the halloumi into four thick slices, then cut them into finger sizes.

Whisk the egg yolks in a bowl. Place some flour and the breadcrumbs in two more separate bowls.

Flour the halloumi pieces, then dip into the egg yolk, then into the breadcrumbs. Ensure they're well coated – you could even do it once more, if desired.

Heat a little sunflower oil in a frying pan until hot, then place the fingers into the pan one by one as you don't want them to overcrowd the pan. Cook until a lovely golden colour, then remove and eat straight away with a bowl of shatta paste. The combination of the creamy, rubbery, salty halloumi with the crispy breadcrumbs and tangy chilli garlic paste is amazing.

Hummus bil shatta

حمص بالشطة

Hummus with spicy shatta

I love hummus, and as you may have noticed I also love chilli. I always used to eat hummus Beiruti, as it is mixed with fresh green chillies and adds a nice kick to a dish, so I thought about how I could make it Palestinian. It's simple – by adding shatta. You'll never use shop-bought chilli paste again.

Serves 4

2 x 400g tins of chickpeas, drained (you can also use dried chickpeas which will have to be soaked overnight – see page 37)
juice of 2 lemons
1 garlic clove, crushed
2 tbsp tahini
1 tbsp Greek yogurt
1 tsp salt
1–2 tsp red Shatta (see opposite)
olive oil, to drizzle

For the hummus, add the chickpeas, lemon juice, garlic, tahini, yogurt and salt to a blender (retain a few whole chickpeas to garnish) and blend to create a smooth paste.

Plate most of the hummus, then swirl the shatta through it. Drizzle over some more hummus and some olive oil, then garnish with the reserved chickpeas in the centre. Not only will it look beautiful but it will taste great.

Overleaf: Market stall in Gaza

From left to right: Makdous; Feta bil zayt

Makdous

مكدوس

Pickled and stuffed baby aubergines

Makdous is eaten all over the Middle East and often served with other dishes, such as a plate of feta cheese, olives, za'atar, sumac and breads. My mum loves it, and I remember her sitting at our dining room table with all of these ingredients and making a meal that looked so simple but which was the absolute essence of home. *Makdous* is a dish of baby aubergines stuffed with a chopped walnut mixture that stays a little crunchy and adds to the texture of the aubergines. It is such an easy dish to make, and also a good one to double up on as the flavours mature over time to become truly fabulous.

You will need

1 sterilized 2.5-litre kilner jar

1.5kg baby aubergines, stalks on but leaves removed (this is easier to do once they have been boiled)

4 litres water

1 red pepper, finely diced

300g walnuts, medium-to-finely crushed

whole head of garlic, cloves peeled and crushed

1 red chilli, finely chopped

olive oil

rock salt

Place the aubergines and water in a large pot, making sure all the aubergines are submerged, and bring to the boil. Cook for about 30 minutes – you want them to soften but not break up. I sometimes put a small plate over them if they are bouncing around too much.

Combine the peppers, nuts, garlic and chilli in a bowl, and use a little olive oil to bind them together. Set aside in the fridge.

When the aubergines are done, place them in a colander, removing any leaves if necessary. Make a slit in each one lengthways from the top to the bottom to create a pocket, but leave them connected – don't cut them in half as you are going to stuff them. Don't cut them too deeply or too close to either edge. Add a little rock salt into each pocket and leave them to drain overnight.

The next day, brush away any remaining salt from the aubergines and fill them generously with the pepper and nut filling, but not so much that it falls out. Clean up the aubergines if necessary with kitchen towel, and place them gently into your kilner jar. Cover them completely with olive oil and seal for a few weeks to allow them to marinate and pickle. The flavours mature and develop over time, so don't be tempted to try them too soon.

Feta bil zayt

جبنة فتا بالزيت

Marinated feta

This is an accompaniment to the *Makdous* recipe opposite. It requires no cooking but is definitely worth putting together. My family and I add chilli to pretty much everything, and it appears here too. The feta submerged in this petrol green oil will literally take on every flavour that is sealed in the jar. I have got tons of jars at home, full of ingredients that have been marinated and stuffed with anything possible, as an option to nibble on when I feel like it.

You will need

1 sterilized 700ml jar

2 tbsp za'atar
1 tsp sumac
1kg feta cheese, cut into
   2.5cm cubes
peel of 1 lemon, cut into
   slivers
1 lemon, cut into small
   wedges
1 tsp pink peppercorns
1 tsp chilli flakes
2 vine leaves, chopped
   (optional)
olive oil

Rub a little of the za'atar and sumac into the feta to catch slightly on the cheese, otherwise it will just float in the oil.

Place the feta into the sterilized jar and add the lemon peel, lemon wedges, peppercorns, chilli flakes and vine leaves, if using. Mix through, then add the olive oil to cover, and leave to marinate for a few weeks. This can be enjoyed after a couple of days, but it just gets better with time.

Right: Old City, Nablus

Above: Ramallah

Salatet bateekh ma' feta

سلطة البطيخ مع جبنة فتا

Watermelon, feta and red onion salad with mint

The ingredients in the title represent everything that Palestinian people enjoy eating: fruits, cheese and onions. Onions play a perfect role here, a sharp hit against the sweetness of the watermelon and the smooth creaminess of the cheese, that's also tart. This will take about three minutes to make, and will remind you of a time when you were on holiday, enjoying the sunshine. It always puts me in a very good mood, remembering all the times I've eaten this with my family, sitting on a balcony, on a beach, or at home after a month of Ramadan, satisfying every tastebud and quenching my thirst.

Serves 4

1 small watermelon
250g good-quality feta
  cheese
½ red onion, cut into half-
  moon slices
handful of fresh mint
  leaves, chopped
1 tbsp caster sugar

Slice the top off the watermelon. Cut slices into the flesh lengthways, then horizontally, and carefully hollow it out by removing the lovely big chunks of flesh with a spoon. If you're lucky your watermelon won't have many seeds, but if it does, try to discard as many as possible. Place the chunks in a large bowl.

Cut the feta cheese into cubes slightly smaller than the melon cubes and mix with the watermelon. Add the red onion slices and mix in.

Combine the mint leaves with the sugar to create a sort of sugared mint. Scatter this all over the salad – you get the sweetness of the sugar, the sharpness of the onion, the creaminess of the cheese, and once again sweetness from the watermelon.

Serve and eat within an hour of cutting the ingredients, otherwise the watermelon starts to lose all its liquid and the salad becomes soggy.

The Fields and Earth

GRAINS AND EARTH-GROWN VEGETABLES

Palestine can almost be split into three sections: the north, with towns and cities such as Akka, Haifa, Al-Nasira (Nazareth), Jenin and Nablus; the central area of Yaffa, El-Lydd, Ramallah, Areeha (Jericho) and of course Al-Quds (Jerusalem); and the most southern part, Beit Lahem (Bethlehem), Al-Khalil (Hebron), Gaza, Ashdod and An-Naqab (Negev). Within each of these areas you will encounter different seasons and landscapes, even though they are all part of the same small country. It is these differences that create the many and varied ingredients that go to make the wide range of wonderful dishes that come from each area.

There is such a diverse habitat that it creates a vast amount of growth all year round. You have a mixture of lush green mountains, coast and desert. In areas such as the West Bank, with the cities of Ramallah, Nablus, Al-Nasira and Akka, grapes, olives and apricots are commonly grown, even in people's backyards. The coastal areas of Gaza and Yaffa are known for their citrus fruits. Herbs and chillies also made their way to the coastal towns through trade routes and influenced the types of food eaten there; dishes from these towns are spicier compared to those in the more northern areas.

In particular, Palestine is a country rich in vegetables, with fertile lands that cross all regions, thanks to the wonderful Mediterranean climate. And with such large movements of people around the country over the years, the cuisines of the different areas have intertwined to create the wonderful, healthy, rich diet that we know as Palestinian.

Dayr Ghazale Village, Jenin

Opposite, clockwise from top: Wadi Fukin, Beit Lahem (Bethlehem); outskirts of Nablus; Al-Rashayida;
This page: Mount of Temptation, Areeha (Jericho)

From left to right: *Bamyeh makliyeh; Muttabal kousa; Muttabal shamandar*

Bamyeh makliyeh

بامية مقلية

Fried okra with chilli

When we were growing up I used to copy my sister Maya in her food likes and dislikes, but as I got older I realized that I enjoyed many more foods than I thought! I love okra, but still have an issue with eating it if it is overcooked, as it can have a gelatinous, slimy texture. So thinking about ingredients that I wanted to keep in my life but eat differently was a way for me to experiment and make them my own. By cooking them this way I managed to keep them crunchy. These are fantastic and so delicious. You will need either fresh or frozen okra – the frozen ones are tiny, like popcorn, so I prefer the bigger, fresh ones as they are more substantial.

Serves 4

2 eggs
150g plain flour
½ tsp paprika
1 tsp chilli flakes
1 tsp ground coriander
1 tsp ground cumin
1 tsp salt
500g fresh or frozen okra,
   tops removed
250ml sunflower oil, for
   frying
squeeze of lemon juice
   (optional)

Whisk the eggs together in a bowl and set aside. In a separate bowl, combine the flour, spices and salt and set aside.

Coat the okra in the eggs and then in the seasoned flour.

Heat the oil in a pan to 180ºC, or until a little flour sizzles when dropped in. Working in batches, add the okra to the oil and fry for a few minutes to let them sizzle, crunch up and turn golden. Remove them from the pan on to kitchen towel to absorb any excess oil, and continue with the remaining batches.

Add a squeeze of lemon, if desired, just to highlight the spices, and serve. Eat them while they are hot so they don't go soggy.

Right: Zababde Village, Jenin

Muttabal shamandar

Roasted beetroot with chilli, yogurt and dill

In Palestine and countries like Syria, *muttabal* of all types of vegetable are popular. I had not eaten this before, however, until I tried it with my friend Saima, and it is now always on my table at home. It is something that I could also see on a table in Gaza, as chilli and dill are so prominent in their cooking.

Serves 4

1kg raw beetroot
500ml thick Greek yogurt
1 red chilli, chopped, or
  chilli flakes
1 large bunch of fresh dill,
  chopped
olive oil, to drizzle
salt

Preheat the oven to 200ºC Fan (220ºC/425ºF/Gas 7).

Rub the beetroot with oil and season with salt, then place in the oven for around 45 minutes until the skin starts to pull away and crack.

Peel the beetroot under cold running water to remove the skin. Cut into small bite-sized pieces, about 1–2cm.

Place the yogurt in a bowl and add the beetroot, chilli and dill. Add a little olive oil, if desired, season with more salt, and serve with your favourite bread.

Muttabal kousa

Smashed courgettes with chilli, yogurt and mint

Courgette *muttabal* is so fresh and light that you will want to make it again and again. I like to chop the courgettes small and sauté them until golden, then add all the other goodies after that. My Mama makes this, and so many other varieties of *muttabal* that they create a rainbow on the table.

Serves 4

100ml olive oil
3 courgettes, cubed
1 garlic clove, crushed
juice of 1 lemon
3 tbsp tahini
2 tbsp Greek yogurt
1 green chilli, chopped
2 tsp dried mint
seeds of 1 pomegranate
salt
Khubez (page 89) or
  Khubez Taboon (page 88)

Heat the olive oil in a pan over a medium heat and sauté the courgettes with 1 teaspoon of salt. Once they have turned a golden caramel colour, remove from the heat and place them in a sieve to drain any excess water.

Smash the courgettes in a bowl with a fork, or pulse them in a food processor – you want a chunky texture, not super smooth. Add the garlic, lemon juice, tahini and yogurt and check for seasoning – add a little more salt, if desired.

Add the chilli and 1 teaspoon of dried mint, mix to combine and place in the fridge to set. Garnish with the pomegranate seeds and remaining mint, and serve with warm toasted pita or taboon bread.

Qallayet bandora

Tangy tomatoes sautéed in olive oil

This is traditionally eaten by farmers to celebrate their olive harvest. You can create this fabulous dish in a simple setting, with a quick outdoor fire and a single pan. It is one of my favourites that I make all the time. The aroma and flavour of the ingredients turn a normal tomato into something else.

Serves 2–4

150ml olive oil, plus extra
   to serve
6 large, ripe plum
   tomatoes, sliced
   lengthways
1–2 garlic cloves
1 large green chilli, crushed
1 heaped tsp dried mint
   (don't use fresh mint as it
   changes the flavour)
salt

Heat the olive oil in a frying pan over a medium heat until hot. Add the tomato slices and let them sizzle – don't move them, as you want them to melt down but not become too 'saucy'. When they have been cooking for about 2–3 minutes, add the garlic and chilli and let them cook down. Season with a little salt.

After about 7–8 minutes, move the ingredients around the pan and stir through half the dried mint. Leave to simmer and thicken for another 12–15 minutes until they start to thicken, resembling the texture of a dip.

Scatter the remaining dried mint on top and serve with extra olive oil.

Qallayet kousa

Courgettes sautéed in olive oil

As with the recipe above, Palestinians are famous for turning any vegetable into a delicious dish, and this really celebrates the ingredients used, such as olive oil and courgette. It is simple, honest food taken directly from the land – no fuss with full flavour.

Serves 2–4

150ml olive oil, plus extra
   to serve
5 medium–large
   courgettes, sliced
1–2 garlic cloves, crushed
1 large green chilli, crushed
1 heaped tsp dried mint
salt

Heat the olive oil in a frying pan until hot. Add the courgette slices and let them sizzle. When they have been cooking for about 2–3 minutes, add the garlic and chilli and let them cook down. Season with a little salt.

After about 7–8 minutes, move the ingredients around the pan and stir through half the dried mint.

Scatter the remaining dried mint on top and serve with extra olive oil.

Caramelized shallots with herby labneh

كراث مشوي مع لبنة بالأعشاب

This dish is a fusion of my experience working in a French restaurant and my home cooking. I love making caramelized shallots, and they taste great with everything. The sweetness against the tartness of the labneh and fresh herbs makes for a great side dish, but they also work well on their own.

Serves 2–4

6 tbsp olive oil
1 tsp cumin seeds
1 tbsp butter
500g banana shallots, peeled
150ml vegetable stock
2–3 tsp honey
2 sprigs of fresh thyme
250g labneh
bunch of fresh flat-leaf parsley, chopped
bunch of fresh dill, chopped
grated zest of 1 lemon
2–4 *Khubez Taboon* (page 88)
salt

Put 2 tablespoons of olive oil and the cumin seeds into a pan over a low heat until they start to release their flavour, about 1–2 minutes, then add the butter and shallots and cook slowly for 7–8 minutes, until they soften slightly and start to colour. Add the vegetable stock and simmer for a few minutes until almost all the stock has been absorbed, then add the honey and thyme and stir constantly until it starts to thicken and get slightly sticky, about 5–7 minutes. Season with a sprinkling of salt and leave to cool.

Mix the labneh with the chopped herbs in a bowl and season with salt. Add the lemon zest to the remaining olive oil in a separate bowl.

Place a little of the labneh onto each of the taboon breads, followed by the caramelized shallots, and drizzle with the lemon oil.

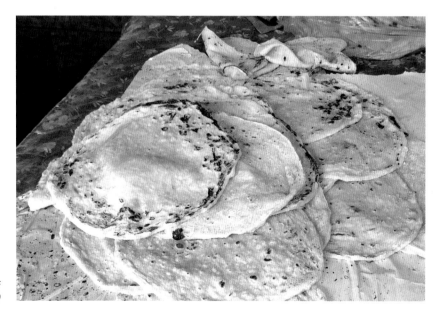

Right: *Old City, Al-Quds (Jerusalem)*

Salatet hummus bil camun

سلطة حمص بالكمون

Cumin and chilli chickpea salad

Serves 4

2 x 400g tins of chickpeas
2 red chillies, chopped
1 red pepper, diced
1 green pepper, diced
1 red onion, finely chopped

For the dressing
2 tbsp red wine vinegar
2 tsp golden caster sugar
4 tbsp ground cumin
150ml olive oil
juice of 1 lemon
small bunch of fresh
 coriander, chopped
1–2 tsp salt

I came up with this dish when I was running my deli, Baity Kitchen, basing it loosely on *Balila* (below), but making it cold, with red peppers, red onions and a sweet vinegar base. The coriander gives it a kick, and the wonderful flavours really complement each other.

Drain and rinse the chickpeas, then place in a large serving bowl with all the chopped vegetables, and stir gently to combine.

Combine all the dressing ingredients in a separate bowl. Toss the dressing through the salad and check for seasoning. This salad gets better as time passes, as the dressing soaks into the chickpeas. It's delicious, sweet, tangy, spicy and earthy.

Auntie Nadia's balila

بليله عمتي ناديا

Cumin chickpeas with spring onions, lemon and olive oil

Serves 4

2 x 400g tins of chickpeas
2 heaped tsp ground cumin
2 garlic cloves, crushed
juice of 1 lemon
2 spring onions, chopped
bunch of fresh flat-leaf
 parsley, chopped
olive oil, to drizzle
1 green chilli, chopped
salt

Balila is so quick to make and reminds me of my trips back to Syria to visit my grandmother. It is thought to have been the forerunner of hummus, but this warm, olive-oil drenched dish of chickpeas with cumin and fresh herbs is probably more of a favourite for me.

Heat the chickpeas in a pan for 5 minutes, then add the cumin and garlic and sauté for another 5 minutes.

Add the lemon juice, spring onions and parsley, and season with salt to taste. Drizzle with lots of olive oil, check the seasoning and stir through the chilli.

Auntie Bushra's harak usba'o

حراق اصبعة من خالتي بشرى

Coriander lentils with fresh pasta and tamarind stew

This dish is most famous in Syria, where my family went as refugees after the Nakba in 1948. It has many similarities to *Rummaniyeh*, which is from Gaza and Yaffa, but this version is slightly elevated due to the fresh coriander and tangy tamarind that run through it. *Harak usba'o* literally means 'he's burnt his finger', perhaps due to the fact that this dish is so delicious that people couldn't wait for it to be ready and ate it straight from a hot pan.

Serves 6–8

760g brown lentils
sunflower oil, for frying
6 medium onions, cut into
 half moons
3 *Khubez* (page 89), cut
 into small squares
6 garlic cloves, crushed
100g tamarind, soaked in
 250ml warm water
2 tbsp pomegranate
 molasses
1 tbsp salt
250g fresh tagliatelle, cut
 into 2.5cm strips
juice of 2–3 lemons
300g fresh coriander
 leaves, chopped
seeds of 1 pomegranate
100ml olive oil

Place the lentils in a pan with enough unsalted water to cover by 5cm, and bring to the boil. Cook for about 40–45 minutes, until thickened and slightly soft. You may need to add a little more water, so do check on them occasionally.

Meanwhile, preheat the oven to 190ºC Fan (210ºC/425ºF/Gas 6–7).

Heat 400ml of sunflower oil in a deep frying pan and cook the onions in batches to caramelize them. This will take about 10–15 minutes per batch.

Bake the bread in the oven for about 10–12 minutes, checking regularly, until golden. Alternatively, fry the bread in a little oil until golden, about 5 minutes.

Add half the caramelized onions and half the garlic to the lentils with the tamarind and pomegranate molasses, and mix to combine. Add the salt and pasta, stir through, and let them cook over a low heat for 3–4 minutes.

Stir in 2 tablespoons of lemon juice and check the seasoning – you may need more lemon juice or salt. Add three-quarters of the coriander and stir through, then transfer to a serving dish.

Mix the remaining garlic with the rest of the coriander. Scatter the bread, coriander, pomegranate seeds and remaining onions in lines over the top of the dish. Drizzle over the olive oil and serve at room temperature.

Above: Biddu Village, outskirts of Al-Quds (Jerusalem)

Kubbeh nayeh bil khudar

كبة نية بالخضار

Vegetables with bulgur wheat, herbs and lemon

Serves 4–6

300g medium bulgur wheat

2 courgettes, cubed

6 tomatoes, cubed

1 onion, diced

2 bunches of fresh chives, finely chopped

large bunch of fresh flat-leaf parsley, chopped

medium bunch of fresh mint, chopped, plus extra to serve

3 tbsp harissa paste or red Shatta (page 42)

juice of 4 lemons

1 fresh green chilli, chopped

300ml olive oil

2–3 tsp salt

Kubbeh nayeh is the Middle East's version of steak tartare; here I am using the same concept but making it with vegetables, combining the spices and bulgur wheat and shaping them like a traditional *kubbeh nayeh*. I first ate this when I visited my friend Hind in Paris. This dish is quite similar in nature to Turkish tabbouleh, and it is a firm favourite in her home in Al-Khalil (Hebron), and has been for centuries. Palestine, like many other countries, has been influenced by so many regions, due to its location, and different ideas have cemented themselves into our culture over time.

Place the bulgur wheat in a bowl and add warm water to cover it by 1cm. Leave to soak for 10 minutes.

Place all the ingredients, including the soaked bulgur wheat, in a separate large bowl and use your hand to really work them together. You want this to almost become the texture of paste, so don't be scared to overwork it. Once you are happy with the texture, taste it and make sure the flavour is to your liking. Bulgur wheat needs plenty of seasoning to really make the flavours stand out. You want this to be tangy, spicy and a little crunchy from the vegetables. I serve it in the shape of traditional flattened kubbeh, with fresh mint in the centre.

This page (top): Nablus; (bottom): Nablus; Opposite: Battir, Beit Lahem (Bethlehem)

From left to right: *Salatet jibneh wa tamer;*
Salatet malfouf bil toum wa na' na';
Salatet bakleh wa rumman

Salatet malfouf bil toum wa na' na'

سلطة ملفوف بالثوم والنعنع

Cabbage salad with cumin, lemon and mint dressing

My Teta used to have this on her dinner table all the time. The mint and cabbage with cumin is such a delicate combination. It is so delicious and fresh, as though you were back home by the sea in Yaffa.

Serves 2–4

½ small white cabbage
2 carrots, grated
1 garlic clove, crushed
2 tsp dried mint
2 tbsp white wine vinegar
1 tsp golden caster sugar
2 tbsp ground cumin
5–10 fresh mint leaves
75–100ml olive oil
juice of 1 lemon
salt, to taste

Finely slice the white cabbage into thin strips, then place all the ingredients in a bowl and mix well to combine, massaging the cabbage with your hands to soften it a little.

Season to taste, and serve straight away.

Salatet jibneh wa tamer

سلطة جبنة وتمر

Soft cheese, date and endive salad

I adore eating anything with dates and I try to incorporate them into as many dishes as I can. There is nothing more Palestinian than our Medjool dates – sticky and gooey, they are the king of dates!

Serves 2–4

300g green endive
120g chèvre cheese
12 Medjool dates, pitted
handful of rocket leaves

For the dressing
100ml balsamic vinegar
300ml olive oil
1 tsp salt
2 tbsp golden caster sugar

Break the endive into pieces and place on a serving plate. Cut the cheese into bite-sized pieces and add to the serving plate with the dates and rocket. Mix everything together gently.

Combine all the ingredients for your dressing, add a squeeze of lemon juice, and drizzle over the salad before serving.

Salatet bakleh wa rumman

سلطة بقلة ورمان

Tangy purslane salad with pomegranate seeds and radish

Bakleh is one of my absolute favourite salad leaves. It has the most delicious flavour – lemony, crunchy and a little peppery – and is full of vitamins. You can cook it, eat it raw or blend it to make a sauce. Here I am using it with two of my other favourite things, pomegranate and radish. A superfood salad.

Serves 2–4

2 large bunches of purslane,
   washed and chopped
   roughly
200g radishes, cut into rings
seeds of 2 pomegranates
bunch of fresh flat-leaf
   parsley, chopped

For the dressing
juice of 2 lemons
2 tbsp apple cider vinegar
150ml olive oil
1 tsp sumac
1 tbsp caster sugar or honey
1 tsp salt

Put the purslane, radishes, pomegranate seeds and parsley into a serving bowl and toss together until well combined.

Combine all the dressing ingredients in a separate bowl and drizzle over the top of the vegetables. The salad cuts through anything fatty, so is a perfect accompaniment to any main course of meat or fish.

Salatet Baba

سلطة بابا

Baba's famous smashed lemon potatoes with spring onions and chilli

My dad loves simple food – especially smashed potatoes. These are reminiscent of mashed potatoes; very garlicky with a hint of chilli. It's all about food that reminds him of home and his mother.

Serves 4–6

1kg potatoes, peeled and
   quartered
juice of 2 lemons
2 heads of garlic, skins
   removed, cloves crushed
1 green chilli, chopped
bunch of fresh flat-leaf
   parsley, roughly chopped
200ml olive oil
pinch of chilli flakes
salt

Bring a large pan of salted water to the boil and boil the potatoes for 10–12 minutes until cooked through. Drain and smash the potatoes, so they still have a little texture.

Add the lemon juice, garlic, green chilli and parsley and mix to combine. Season with salt, drizzle with the olive oil and scatter over the chilli flakes. Serve with *Qallayet Bandora* (page 60) and some warm bread.

Batata bil leymoun wa bassal akhdar

بطاطا وليمون وبصل أخضر

Lemon, spring onion and dill potatoes

I learnt this dish from a friend's father and fell in love with it. The tangy lemon goes so well with everything. We have similar flavours running through our food, which makes it easy to combine dishes.

Serves 4–6

1.1kg potatoes, such as
   King Edward, skin on
2 spring onions, chopped
bunch of fresh dill, chopped
juice of 1½ lemons
150ml olive oil
2 tsp salt
pinch of black pepper
1 tbsp plain flour

Preheat the oven to 200ºC Fan (220ºC/475ºF/Gas 7). Cut the potatoes into wedges and place them into a baking tray with half the spring onions and dill, the lemon juice, olive oil, salt, pepper and flour. Mix everything together and place in the oven for 60–75 minutes, until the potatoes have browned.

Remove from the oven, add the remaining dill and spring onions and serve.

Khudar mashwi bil za'atar wa shatta

خضار مشوية بالزعتر والشطة

Tray bake of za'atar roasted vegetables and shatta drizzle

When you have a big family, roasting vegetables takes the stress out of cooking, as it all goes into the oven in one tray so you can focus on other things. Although prepping and cleaning may take time, my Mama used to make this in big batches and we would always have more for the next day. You can also prepare the vegetables in advance. This is comforting to eat and is accompanied by shatta, a spicy Palestinian dip, as chilli is never far away in any of our foods. We have such fabulous land and agriculture throughout Palestine that our vegetables never go unnoticed and are often the star of a meal. You can use any root vegetables you like here.

Serves 6–8

2 large carrots, each cut lengthways into 4
1 swede, cut into similar-sized chunks as carrot
2 beetroot, cut into chunks
2 sweet potatoes, cut into lengths
2 courgettes, cut into lengths
2 red onions, quartered
whole head of garlic, halved
1 tsp salt
2–3 tsp za'atar
generous drizzle of olive oil
red Shatta (page 42), to drizzle

Preheat the oven to 200°C Fan (220°C/475°F/Gas 7).

Make sure the vegetables are cut into similar-sized pieces for even cooking. Mix everything together in a roasting tray, season with the salt and za'atar, and drizzle generously with olive oil. Roast in the oven for about 60–70 minutes. I turn them every once in a while to caramelize them equally and ensure they cook evenly.

When you're happy with the colour and feel of them – I prefer mine with a slight crunch – remove from the oven and drizzle with the shatta while they are still hot. Serve immediately.

Right: *Nisf Jubeil, Nablus*

Silek bil sumac wa laymoun / wa tahineh

سلق بالسماق والليمون / والطحينة

Sautéed Swiss chard two ways: with lemon and sumac / with tahini

Silek is a beautiful dark green leaf, which works really well stuffed and added to salads or stews. I think families favoured dishes that were quick to put together because of the large numbers they had to feed.

Serves 4

400g Swiss chard
olive oil
2 large onions, diced
1 garlic clove, crushed
juice of 1–2 lemons
1 heaped tsp sumac
2–3 tbsp tahini
1 tsp salt

Wash the Swiss chard, then separate the stalks from the leaves and chop both stalks and leaves. Heat 75ml olive oil in a deep pot over a low heat, and sauté the onions until soft. Add the garlic and continue to cook until the flavours come out, about 5–7 minutes. Add the chopped Swiss chard stalks and cook for 10 minutes to soften, then add the leaves and cook until wilted.

Add the lemon and sumac *or* the tahini (to your desired taste) and stir to combine. Season with salt, drizzle over a little olive oil and serve.

Ful wa artichoke bil kuzbara

فول وارض الشوكة بالكزبرة

Artichokes and green broad beans with coriander, garlic and lemon

This dish is so fresh and tangy and really reminds me of summer. My Mama loves this dish. It is so vibrant and green and can be cooked all year round, as she uses frozen broad beans and artichokes.

Serves 4–6

1 x 500g packet of frozen
  green broad beans
1 x 500g packet of frozen
  artichoke hearts
1 tbsp caster sugar
olive oil
4 garlic cloves, crushed
large bunch of fresh
  coriander, chopped
juice of 2 lemons
salt

Begin by cooking the beans in salted water for about 30 minutes. At the same time, add the frozen artichokes to a separate pan of boiling water and simmer with the sugar until tender, about 30–40 minutes. They are ready when they become slightly soft, which is what you are looking for.

While they are cooking, place 200ml of olive oil into a pan with the garlic and sauté for about 2 minutes to combine all the flavours. You don't want to caramelize anything, you just want to create an infused warm oil.

Drain the beans and artichokes. Cut the cooked artichokes into 2cm pieces, and combine the beans and artichokes with the garlic oil in a serving bowl. Add the coriander, drizzle with lemon juice and check for seasoning. Drizzle with olive oil, and serve warm.

The Bakery

SAVOURY PASTRIES

Mahmoud Darwish wrote so prolifically and passionately about our land and our bread that he became a symbol of hope to the Palestinian people. Bread creates an appetite for life, and no Palestinian home would be the same without *Khubez* (page 89) or *Khubez Taboon* (page 88) on the table.

Bread is everywhere in Palestine; the most wonderful smells waft through the streets all over the country, and bakeries are the focus of everyday life. They are all over the place, and people queue daily to get their fresh bread and pastries. My Teta Najla used to tell my mother of how she would prepare her dough, then take it to the town baker (*furn il baladi*), who would prove it and bake it for her as she didn't have enough space in her kitchen while she was preparing everything else for her eleven children. There is a sense of community among the bakers and their customers, which is something you don't find in many other countries.

The different types of breads and stuffings are simply wonderful, but I have to say that I prefer to make my own, as do my mother, her sisters and my father's sisters, all of whom are pretty much master bakers, having learned to prepare everything themselves. My favourite bread is probably anything with cheese, za'atar and olive oil, as these just represent Palestine to me. This chapter contains many traditional pastry recipes, but I have added some of my own twists, as I love playing around with dough and creating new ideas – I think my Teta would be proud.

Al-Quds (Jerusalem) market

*This page, all images: Ramallah; **Opposite (top):** Al Rahaweh, north of Al-Khalil (Hebron); **(bottom):** Jenin market*

From left to right: Mai's Akkawi bread; Khubez; Khubez taboon

Khubez taboon

خبز طابون

Palestinian taboon bread

We eat taboon bread alongside pretty much anything! It should be soft and pillowy, so be sure to watch out for it while cooking. This would usually be cooked in a clay oven called a taboon, but can easily be made without – you just may not get all the bubbles you would when it is cooked in the traditional way. Some people bake it on hot stones to recreate this effect, but the reality is we don't all have such things floating around our kitchens.

Makes 6

300g plain flour, plus extra
    for rolling out
200g bread flour
1 x 7g sachet instant yeast
1 tsp caster sugar
1 tbsp salt
350ml warm water
3–4 tbsp olive oil

Combine all the ingredients and mix until a dough forms. Knead for a few minutes until the dough is soft and bouncy, then set aside in a well-oiled bowl, covered with a tea towel, for 30–45 minutes.

Once risen, divide the mixture into six balls, then roll each one out on a floured surface. Roll them out quite thinly as this will help with the bubbling, fluffy effect you are after.

Place a dry frying pan over a medium heat, then cook the flattened dough one piece at a time, for 1–2 minutes each side. As soon as you see them puffing up and browning slightly, turn them over and cook the other side. They should be fluffy and soft when cooked.

These can be dipped in za'atar, or served with the Garlic Labneh (page 26), the Caramelized Shallots (page 63) – or as an accompaniment to most dishes!

Mai's Akkawi bread

خبز عكاوي على طريقة مي

I met an amazing lady called Mai on social media, and loved her posts so much, so she kindly gave me this recipe to share with you. This shows up on my dinner table every few weeks, as it is so good and so moreish. You can stuff it with anything you like, but Akkawi cheese and za'atar are my favourites.

Makes 18

2 x 7g sachets instant yeast
240–250ml warm water
1 tbsp caster sugar
480g plain flour
1 tsp salt
125ml vegetable oil
190ml olive oil
170–225g Akkawi cheese (or any salty white cheese, such as feta or halloumi)
75g za'atar
labneh, to serve

Mix the yeast with 240ml warm water and the sugar until it bubbles, about 5–10 minutes. Preheat the oven to 160ºC Fan (180ºC/350ºF/Gas 4).

Sift the flour into a bowl and add the salt. Add the yeast mixture to the flour and slowly drizzle in the vegetable oil and 125ml olive oil. Mix the dough until it pulls away from the sides of the bowl, adding a little more water if needed. Knead for about 5–7 minutes; it won't be as 'bouncy' as regular dough, as it has plenty of oil in it, so don't be alarmed. Leave to rest for 40 minutes.

Make golf-ball-sized pieces of dough and stuff each ball with a little of the cheese.

Mix the za'atar with the remaining olive oil and rub each dough ball in the oil to coat them evenly. Place the dough balls into a bundt tin, cover with a tea towel and leave to rise for another 20 minutes. Bake for 20–30 minutes until golden and puffed up. Serve with labneh.

Khubez

خبز كماج

Pita bread

Khubez plays a part in almost every Palestinian meal. I use it to scoop *molokhia* (a stew made with the leafy green), *Harak Usba'o* (page 66), dips and rice dishes. It is simple to make and always better than store-bought. I like to change it up with sesame seeds sometimes, as they are so good for you.

Serves 8

1 x 7g sachet instant yeast
240ml warm water
1 tsp golden caster sugar
400g plain flour
50ml olive oil, plus extra to drizzle
sesame seeds

Mix the yeast and warm water together in a large bowl. Leave for a couple of minutes, then add the sugar and stir through. Add the flour and olive oil and knead together until you have a smooth dough. This should take 5–8 minutes. Leave the dough to rise in an oiled bowl, covered with a tea towel, for about 1 hour.

Preheat the oven to 220ºC Fan (240ºC/465ºF/Gas 9). Cut the dough into eight equal pieces and shape them into balls. Place them on a baking tray and leave to rise for 10 minutes. Once risen, flatten each ball slightly to a pita shape, then leave for another 5 minutes. Bake for 5 minutes, or until the pitas have puffed up, then drizzle with olive oil and sprinkle each one with 1–2 teaspoons of sesame seeds.

Sadia's khubez falaheen

خبز فلاحين من عمتي سعدية

Homemade flattened pastry with fresh za'atar leaves

This bread is eaten throughout Palestine, but most commonly in rural areas where people collected fresh za'atar from their land and cooked batches of this on open fires. This bread is quick to make and absolutely delicious as it incorporates Palestine's two most important flavours: za'atar and olive oil.

Serves 4–8

800g plain flour
350ml water
1 tsp salt
1 tsp golden caster sugar
1 x 7g sachet instant yeast
olive oil, for rolling out and
    drizzling

For the stuffing
5 tbsp olive oil
1 onion, finely chopped
45g fresh za'atar or
    oregano, finely chopped
1 tbsp sumac
1 tbsp salt

In a bowl, combine the flour, water, salt, sugar and yeast and mix until a dough forms. Knead for about 5 minutes until soft and bouncy. Place in a bowl, cover with a tea towel, and set aside to rise for 40 minutes.

While the dough is rising, combine all the stuffing ingredients in a bowl.

Cut the dough into four pieces. Using a little oil on your hands and work surface, flatten one piece out with your hands to a very thin layer; don't worry if it rips as it will be folded over. Once you have spread it out to about 25–30cm, take a handful of the stuffing mixture and spread it down the centre of the dough. Fold one long side over the stuffing, and then fold over the other side. Spread with a tiny bit more stuffing, and then fold the pastry over the stuffing from the top and bottom ends. Press down to make a secure parcel. Set aside while you repeat this process with the remaining dough and filling.

Preheat the oven to its highest temperature setting. Line two large baking trays with baking parchment and place the pieces of dough on the trays, using your hand to flatten them out slightly. The thinner you get them, the crispier they will be. Bake for 10–12 minutes until golden brown.

Remove from the oven and drizzle with olive oil, then serve for breakfast with some mint tea. Simple and delicious.

Khubez bil za'atar / Khubez bil feta wa shatta

خبز بالزعتر / خبز جبنة بالفتا والشطة

Za'atar brioche twists / Feta brioche twists

When I ran my deli, I had the most amazing man working for me. He was very unorthodox in his baking and I was intrigued. He never measured anything, just did it all by eye, which was quite simply mesmerizing. For me, baking is quite technical and very precise. I would watch him like a hawk, thinking 'this is never going to work', and then a few hours later he would present me with the most amazing cakes, desserts, breads and bakes. This is one of his recipes that I finally managed to get him to weigh out (although it has been scaled down). It is so delicious as a basic dough, but of course I have added my flavourings to make it taste like home.

Makes 2 loaves

120ml full-fat milk, warmed

1 x 7g sachet instant yeast

500g plain flour, sifted
  twice

2 large eggs

1 tsp Himalayan pink salt
  (or coarse sea salt)

90g salted butter, at room
  temperature, cut into
  cubes

Za'atar filling
100g za'atar

100ml olive oil

1 tsp chilli flakes

Cheese filling
1 x 200g packet of feta
  cheese, crumbled

4 tbsp red Shatta (page 42)

handful of chopped fresh
  flat-leaf parsley

To make the dough, mix the milk and yeast together well, then add the flour, eggs and salt and combine. Mix in the butter well and keep mixing the dough until it is firm. If it is too dry, add more milk, 1 tablespoon at a time; if it is too wet, add 1 tablespoon of flour at a time. The dough should be quite dense and heavy. Mix for about 5 minutes in total.

I also like to knead the dough for a minute or two, just to feel it in my hands, to make sure I know it is ready. It should have a little bounce to it.

Place in an oiled bowl and leave to rise for about 45 minutes, then transfer to the fridge for a minimum of 4–6 hours, but overnight is best.

Cut the chilled dough into two pieces and roll it out into two long rectangle shapes (about the size of A4 paper, or even a little bigger).

In separate bowls, combine the ingredients for the two fillings.

Spread one filling over one of the rectangles and roll the dough into a sausage shape from the longest edge. Turn the dough so the short edge is at the top of your work surface, and slice it all the way down the middle so you have two long pieces. Gently begin to wrap them around each other, making sure the filling side is facing upwards to show what's inside. This will create a wonderful shape, and when it bakes it will look beautiful. Repeat with the other rectangle and filling.

Line two 900g loaf tins with baking parchment and place one loaf in each tin. Let them rise for a further 90 minutes in a warm place to fluff up slightly. If you don't, it may result in an uncooked dough and be very dense.

Preheat the oven to 170ºC Fan (190ºC/375ºF/Gas 5). When ready, place in the oven for about 30–40 minutes until golden brown.

Khubez bil awermah wa bayd

خبزة قاورما بالبيض

Pastry stuffed with spiced lamb with eggs

Awermah is a preserved meat that is cooked low and slow with *liyeh*, a fat from fat-tailed lambs. You can, however, use any type of lamb fat you can find, as it is not possible to find *liyeh* easily outside of the Middle East. You could also use duck fat, as this works beautifully too. *Awermah* is slightly seasoned and used in many dishes, such as *hummus bil awermah*, *bayd ma' awermah*, and stuffed into breads. This batch is relatively small, but you can double it up if you like.

Serves 4–6

You will need
1 sterilized 500ml jar

For the awermah
360ml water
1kg fat from lamb meat, roughly chopped (or use duck fat)
2½ tsp rock salt
500g lean lamb meat, chopped into 1cm pieces
1 tsp allspice

For the dough
500g plain flour
1 tsp sea salt
100g butter, softened
1 egg yolk
150ml buttermilk
200ml water

4–6 eggs
sumac, to sprinkle
fresh coriander leaves, to sprinkle

For the *awermah*, pour the water into a heavy-based pan, then add the fat. Adding the water will prevent the fat from sticking to the bottom of the pan while melting. Add the salt and cook the lamb fat over a medium heat until it melts, then add the meat and allspice and cook for about 1 hour, until it has all cooked through thoroughly. Leave to cool completely, place in a sterilized jar and keep in the fridge for up to one month.

While the lamb is cooking, make the dough. This quantity is enough for quite a few of these, but you don't have to use it all; you can reserve some for the freezer and use at another time. Rub the flour, salt and butter together until it resembles breadcrumbs. Add the egg yolk, buttermilk and water and combine. Knead until you have a slightly smooth dough, then wrap in clingfilm and place in the fridge until needed.

Preheat the oven to 170ºC Fan (190ºC/375ºF/Gas 5). Divide the dough into four to six pieces and press out into circles, making them quite thin (about the thickness of a 50p piece) and around 15cm in diameter. Add some of the meat mixture in a line going all the way around the edge, and fold the dough over; you can either press with a fork or make a curved pattern as I have done.

Transfer to a floured baking tray, place in the oven and cook for about 7–8 minutes then take them out. Break an egg into the centre of each one, then return to the oven for a further 3–4 minutes to cook the egg through. I like my eggs slightly runny, but you can cook them for a little longer, if desired. Sprinkle with a little sumac and coriander, and serve straight away.

From left to right: *Fatayer jibneh / lahmeh / sabanekh*

Above: *Jenin market*

Fatayer lahmeh / jibneh / sabanekh

فطاير لحمة / جبنة / سبانخ

Meat and onion pasties / Three-cheese and nigella seed pasties /
Spinach, sumac and onion pasties

You will find these delicately spiced pasties in almost every food shop in Palestine – they are eaten for breakfast, lunch and dinner. They also make fantastic snacks to have on hand whenever you are feeling peckish. The dough is soft, with a variety of fillings, and once cooked can be frozen for another time. My Auntie Muntaha is one of the best bakers in our family, and this is her recipe.

Makes 40–45

For the dough
1.2kg plain flour
600ml water
2 x 7g sachets instant yeast
50g caster sugar
1 tsp salt
120ml olive oil

2 eggs, beaten, to egg wash
pomegranate seeds, to serve
chopped fresh flat-leaf parsley, to serve
lemon wedges, to serve

Whisk half of the flour with the water, yeast, sugar and salt, and set aside for 20 minutes to activate the yeast. Once you see some bubbles, add the remaining flour and oil and mix to combine, then knead the dough for about 5 minutes. Leave to rise, covered with a tea towel, for 40 minutes, then divide the dough into golf-ball-sized pieces and flatten them into rounds.

Preheat the oven to 180ºC Fan (200ºC/400ºF/Gas 6). In a bowl, combine the ingredients for your chosen stuffing.

Add a little of the filling to each piece of dough and shape them to your liking. I pinch two ends to make boat shapes, or fold the dough over the filling on three sides to make triangle shapes. You can make square shapes, round shapes – it's up to you! Press the edges together firmly so they don't open up too much during cooking, since the dough is very fluffy and soft. Egg wash the sides and bake on a lined baking sheet for 12–15 minutes until golden. Scatter the meat and onion pasties with pomegranate seeds and parsley, and serve with a few lemon wedges.

For the cheese filling:
100g halloumi cheese; 100g feta cheese; 100g kaskawan cheese (or use more halloumi or feta); 1 egg; 1 tsp plain flour; 10g chopped fresh flat-leaf parsley; 1 tsp salt; 1 tsp cracked black pepper; 1 tsp nigella sativa seeds

For the spinach, sumac and onion filling:
400g spinach, chopped; 2 onions, chopped; 1 tsp salt; 1 tsp sumac; ½ tsp chilli flakes; 2 tbsp olive oil; juice of 2 lemons

For the meat and onion filling:
1 onion, puréed; 1 green chilli, chopped; 1 tomato, diced; 1 tsp salt; 1 tsp cracked black pepper; 1 garlic clove, smashed; 2 tbsp Greek yogurt; 300g lamb mince; 3 tbsp pomegranate molasses; 1 tsp paprika

Spicy sujuk puffs
with sesame seeds

Sujuk is a delicious spiced lamb sausage that we use in many breakfast dishes, and also in pastry. I prefer to make my own *sujuk* meat mixture because I can choose the flavours I want to be more exaggerated. I also usually love to make my own pastry, but life is too short to make puff pastry, so I use ready-made all-butter puff pastry, which is fabulous. The dish has its origins in Armenia, Turkey and Lebanon, with changes made here and there as it has travelled, to suit the flavours of each country.

Makes 12–14

1 x 320g packet of shop-
   bought, ready-rolled
   all-butter puff pastry
2 beaten eggs, to egg
   wash
handful of sesame seeds,
   to sprinkle

For the filling

1 tsp paprika
1 tsp ground coriander
1 tsp ground cumin
1 tsp dried chilli flakes
1 tsp ground cinnamon
½ tsp ground nutmeg
1½ tsp sea salt
1 garlic clove, finely
   chopped
1 onion, finely chopped
1 tbsp pomegranate
   molasses
400g lamb mince

Combine all the filling ingredients in a bowl. You can add more or less of the spices if you like – it is totally up to you. I sometimes add extra chilli, garlic and pomegranate molasses, according to my mood. When you are happy with your flavourings, set the bowl aside.

Lay out the pre-rolled pastry to create a large rectangle and place some of the filling in a sausage shape along one long edge. Roll the pastry over the meat, just to cover it, then egg wash the edge to seal it, brush the top with egg, and sprinkle the log with sesame seeds. Cut the log away from the rest of the pastry and place on a baking sheet lined with baking parchment. Continue filling, rolling, sealing, sprinkling and cutting until you have used up all the mixture. You should have 3–4 long logs of pastry-covered meat. If you have any filling left over you can always freeze it and use it in other recipes. Place the logs in the fridge to firm up for 20 minutes.

Preheat the oven to 200ºC Fan (220ºC/425ºF/Gas 7). Place the refrigerated logs in the oven and cook for 25–35 minutes until the meat is cooked through and the pastry is golden. Cut and serve in single portions.

Auntie Fathiyeh's zungol / zunkul

زنكول عمتي فتحية

Thin pastry stuffed with minced meat, spices and herbs

This recipe is famous on my father's side of the family, as my Teta Huda loved to bake. *Zongol, zunkul, zongul* – however you choose to spell it – is simply a thin pastry wrapped around delicately spiced meats, quickly fried and eaten straight away. It does take some time to make, but it is well worth it. A taste of Safad in your hands.

Makes 6–8

500g plain flour
180g Greek yogurt
165ml warm milk
1 x 7g sachet instant yeast
½ tsp fennel seeds
2 tsp sesame seeds
1 tsp black sesame seeds
1 tsp caster sugar
1 tsp salt
500ml sunflower oil, for
  frying, plus a little extra
  for greasing

For the filling

150ml olive oil
3 onions, finely diced
250g lamb mince
1 tsp cracked black pepper
1 tsp salt
1 tsp ground cinnamon
1 tsp sumac
1 tbsp pomegranate
  molasses

Combine the flour, yogurt, milk, yeast, seeds, sugar and salt for about 5 minutes in a stand mixer – or by hand for about 10–12 minutes – then set aside and let it rise for an hour.

While the dough is rising, heat 100ml of olive oil in a pan over a medium–low heat and cook the onions until they are translucent. In a separate pan (at the same time), cook off the meat in the remaining olive oil with the spices until slightly browned. Both should take about 15 minutes.

Once cooked, add them together, along with the pomegranate molasses, and mix well to combine all the flavours, then leave to cool.

Cut the dough into balls of no more than 65g. Spread each ball out on a well-greased surface, then use your fingers to spread it out to a very thin pastry. Mine was about 15–20cm wide, with a few tears here and there. Those don't matter as you will be folding them over.

Cut each piece of rolled out dough in half and place some meat mixture lengthways in the centre. Fold the long sides over the meat, then fold in the short sides to seal the meat and press down to make sure they don't open. You want to make rectangle shapes that are well sealed.

Heat the oil in a deep frying pan to 180°C. Make sure it is not too hot as it will cook and burn the outside without cooking the inside, and you will have a soggy pastry. Place the pastries in the hot oil in batches, and fry just until golden, flipping once to colour both sides; the meat is already cooked, so they don't need too long. Remove from the oil and drain on kitchen towel for a few minutes. Serve and eat straight away.

Above: Qabatiya Town, Jenin

Shishbarak

Meat-filled dumplings in a yogurt sauce

These beautiful little dumplings stuffed with minced lamb and onions are so delicious, you simply want to eat them all. Thought to have originated in Turkey, Iran and Iraq, each of which has a different variation, they have travelled through to Palestine over the centuries and become one of our staples. The Iranian name for them is *gosh e-barreh* – lambs' ears – which I think is very cute. If preferred, you can halve this recipe, but I would make it as specified and keep the rest in the freezer for the next time you want to eat this, as it takes a little time to make.

Serves 8

100ml sunflower oil
500g fine lamb mince
1 tsp cracked black pepper
½ tsp ground cinnamon
2 onions, finely chopped
600g plain flour
350ml water
500g Greek yogurt
550ml lamb stock
bunch of fresh coriander, chopped
3 garlic cloves, smashed
150ml olive oil
salt

Place half the sunflower oil in a pan and the other half in a second pan and set both over a medium–low heat. Brown the minced lamb meat in one pan with the black pepper, cinnamon and 1 teaspoon of salt, and add the onions to the second pan to soften and cook down.

While these are cooking, place the flour, water and 1 tablespoon of salt into a stand mixer (or do it by hand), and mix until the dough has come together and is soft and smooth. Set the dough aside to rest.

Once the meat has cooked and the onions have softened, about 10–12 minutes, combine them in a bowl and leave to cool. You want the mixture to be cold when placing it in the dough.

Preheat the oven to 180ºC Fan (200ºC/400ºF/Gas 6). Roll out the dough to the thickness of a 50p piece and cut out circles that are about the size of a 50p piece. You don't want them too thin or too thick. Place a piece of dough between your fingers to flatten it slightly, add a tiny amount of stuffing and seal the edges together by pressing down to create a crescent shape. Now turn it over so the crescent is facing downwards and twist the dough to attach the two ends together, over your index finger, to create a little dumpling. Repeat with the remaining dough and filling and place them one by one on a floured surface. If using the whole recipe, you could get over 200 pieces.

Place them on a baking tray in the oven for 5 minutes to harden them a little. If you are not using them all now, freeze some at this stage for future use.

Place the yogurt and stock in a pan and heat gently to combine. Meanwhile, combine the coriander and smashed garlic together in a bowl, add the olive oil and set aside until you are ready to serve.

Place your *shishbarak* in the yogurt sauce and cook for about 10 minutes until cooked all the way through and the filling is hot. Place in a serving bowl, drizzle with the coriander-garlic mix, and enjoy.

The Farm

ANIMALS

People often ask me why many of the dishes in our cuisine use lamb instead of beef, and the answer my mother gave was that cows were much more expensive to buy, and lamb was the cheaper and more traditional meat. Lamb is very important to us and holds a place of honour at our dinner table, and the slaughter of a lamb is a ritual that is still held today, a sacrifice during celebrations and as a historical tradition.

In areas such as Safad, Akka and Al-Nasira (Nazareth), people traditionally ate more goat, and heavier dishes were introduced. Lebanon has a huge influence on the food in that particular area, as it is in such close proximity.

Nowadays my family eats both beef and lamb, but lamb is still the more dominant presence. Our land is fertile, green and lush, with crops for the animals to graze on; as you travel across the country, you will pass by many villages where the animals are outdoors, and cared for organically. Farmers look after their animals like family, as they do their trees and crops, as this is their sustenance. It is what keeps them alive and nourished.

Palestinians cook their animals with love and pride, and I hope you will get a sense from the recipes in this chapter that not only is the meat prepared with lots of care and attention, but the spices and herbs are used beautifully, to highlight the meat and the meal itself.

Al Zababdeh, Jenin

This page: Sunset hike, Al-Khalil (Hebron) to Al-Rashayida;
Opposite (top): *Ya'bad Village;* **(bottom):** *Al-Zababdeh, Jenin*

*From left to right: Auntie Majeda's
Daoud Basha; Vermicelli rice*

Auntie Majeda's Daoud Basha

داوود باشا من عمتي ماجدة

Lamb meatballs in a tamarind and tomato sauce with caramelized onions

This dish probably originated in Lebanon or Syria. Since my grandmothers fled to Syria after the Nakba in 1948, their food was influenced by the many cuisines surrounding them, as there were refugees from other neighbouring countries. This dish is said to be named after a high-ranking Ottoman official called Daoud Basha, who is thought to have ruled over Lebanon and Iraq during that time. True or not, the dish is delicious and, as with every family, we all have our own version; this one is laced in tamarind, which is simply exquisite next to the lamb meatballs.

Serves 6–8

600g lamb mince
6 onions: 1 finely diced, and 5 cut into half-moon slices
3 tsp salt
1 tsp cracked black pepper
2 tbsp sunflower oil
1 litre smooth tomato passata
5 tbsp tamarind liquid (easy to find in most ethnic stores)
Vermicelli Rice (page 116)

Preheat the oven to 180ºC Fan (200ºC/400ºF/Gas 6). Combine the lamb mince with the finely diced onion, 1 teaspoon salt and the pepper, mixing well. Make golf-ball-sized balls with the meat and place them on a baking sheet in the oven to seal them and turn them brown, about 15 minutes.

While they are cooking, sauté the half moon onions in the sunflower oil for 10–15 minutes until they are slightly caramelized. Once ready, add the tomato passata, the tamarind and remaining salt, and let it cook down for about 15–20 minutes on a medium–high heat.

Take the meatballs out of the oven and add them to the tomato tamarind mix with all their juices. Simmer for a further 30 minutes to really incorporate the flavours. Serve with vermicelli rice.

Right: Ein Karem, Al-Quds (Jerusalem)

Rasmiyeh's kubbeh bil laban

كبة باللبن من عمتي رسمية

Lamb and bulgur kubbeh in a yogurt sauce

Serves 6–8

500g bulgur wheat
750g lamb mince
1 onion, finely grated
½ tsp each of ground
    cinnamon, ground cumin
    and black pepper
½ small green chilli,
    chopped
2 sprigs of fresh mint,
    chopped
2 tsp dried marjoram
sunflower oil
olive oil

For the stuffing
4 onions, diced
500g lamb mince
1 tsp cracked black pepper
½ tsp ground cinnamon
1 tsp dried marjoram
1 tsp salt

For the vermicelli rice
5 vermicelli nests, crushed
350g Egyptian rice
625ml water
2 tsp salt

For the yogurt mix
500g Greek yogurt
1 egg white
1 tbsp cornflour mixed with
    3 tbsp cold water
2 tsp salt

**For the coriander
    garlic oil**
3 garlic cloves, smashed
20g fresh coriander,
    chopped

Everything about this is delicious. The contrast of the tender yet crunchy meat patties in the creamy yogurt sauce with the zingy coriander garlic oil is fantastic and will always leave you wanting more.

For the stuffing, heat 150ml of sunflower oil in a pan and sauté the onions until softened, then add the lamb mince, spices, herbs and salt and sauté for 10–12 minutes until browned and cooked through. Set aside to cool down.

Make the outer casing mixture by combining the bulgur, lamb, onion, spices, chilli, herbs and 2 teaspoons of olive oil. Knead the mixture until it is soft but still firm enough to work with. Divide the mixture into golf-ball-sized balls, then dip your finger into a bowl of cold water and push your finger into the middle of one ball to create a thin, hollow rugby ball shape that is open at one end. Add a heaped teaspoon of the stuffing and close the hole using your fingers and thumb. If this is difficult, you can make a round shape and it will still work. Repeat with the rest of the balls, and refrigerate until you are ready to cook. They can also be frozen for later use (defrost them thoroughly before cooking).

For the rice, heat 4 tablespoons of sunflower oil in a pan and sauté the vermicelli until caramel coloured; watch it carefully, as it turns very quickly and can burn easily. Add the rice and mix to combine, then add the water and salt and cook over a high heat for 3–4 minutes, before reducing the heat to medium–low and cooking for a further 15–20 minutes.

Place all the ingredients for the yogurt mix in a pan and heat through, stirring, until thickened, about 5 minutes. Strain into a bowl to remove any lumps.

Lightly sauté the garlic and coriander in 2 tablespoons of olive oil, tossing the garlic and coriander through the oil to combine.

Half-fill a deep pan with sunflower oil and heat the oil to 180ºC. Do not let it get too hot as the kubbeh may break up if they are moving around too much. Cook them in batches in the oil for 3–4 minutes, turning once, until they are a dark golden brown. Remember you are only cooking through the outside as the inner mixture is already cooked. When the kubbeh are ready, remove from the oil and drain on kitchen towel for a few minutes.

Place them in the yogurt mixture and drizzle the coriander garlic oil over the top. Serve with the vermicelli rice.

Auntie Najwa's kubbeh nayeh

كبة نية من خالتي نجوى

Raw minced lamb with delicate spices

I love going to the butcher with my Mama. She literally stands over him while he is cutting, grinding or slicing her meat, talking about how much more he should be cleaning off the fat, that it should be like this or that – she wants it perfect, and for this dish it has to be, as you are eating raw meat. When she makes this she asks for meat from the leg or shoulder that has been totally stripped of fat or sinew. The meat is literally the star of the show, and its freshness and how many times it is minced is really important. She minces it three times to make sure that it is very fine and workable with her hands. The recipe below is simply a guide in terms of spices – please feel free to use as much or as little seasoning as you want. This is the Middle East's version of steak tartare, and it is divine!

Serves 2–4

500g very finely minced lamb shoulder, fat and sinew totally removed (ask your butcher to grind it 3 times – it should resemble a paste)
1 tsp ground cinnamon
2 tsp ground cumin
1 tsp cracked black pepper
2 tsp dried marjoram
1–2 tsp salt
150g very fine bulgur wheat
1 onion, chopped
½ red chilli, finely chopped
½ red pepper, roughly chopped
75ml olive oil, plus extra to drizzle
2–3 sprigs of fresh mint leaves, plus extra to serve
Khubez Taboon (page 88), onions and radishes, to serve

Place the meat and all the spices, herbs and salt into a bowl and mix well. Add the bulgur wheat and mix to combine.

Place the onion, chilli, red pepper, olive oil and mint into a food processor and blitz to create a smooth paste. Mix this into the meat and bulgur mix, then work this with your hands for about 5 minutes, if not more, to make sure you have a putty-like consistency.

Check for seasoning, adding more of anything you prefer; this is just my way of making it. When happy with the taste, place it in the fridge until ready to serve.

Drizzle with olive oil, top with a few sprigs of fresh mint, and enjoy. Serve with taboon bread, freshly cut onions and radishes.

Ruz wa bazela/ Ruz bil ful

أرز وبازيلاء / أرز بالفول

Lamb and Egyptian rice with cinnamon, nutmeg
and peas / green broad beans

When we were young this dish was always present as it didn't take too long to make. I have included two versions here as you can literally swap the peas for the beans, if you like. *Ruz wa bazela* was a childhood favourite of mine and still is. I love the meat and rice mixture with the spices and the peas, served with buttered pine nuts. We prefer the peas, but my Mama loves the *ful*. Try both and decide which is your favourite…

Serves 4–6

200g frozen peas or broad
  beans
70ml sunflower oil
200g lamb mince
1 tsp salt
1 tsp cracked black pepper
450g Egyptian rice
1 tsp ground cinnamon
1 tsp grated nutmeg
650ml water
25g butter
70g pine nuts
1 x quantity Yogurt Dip
  (page 178)

If using frozen broad beans, boil them in water for 25 minutes and drain.

Heat the oil in a pan, then add the lamb mince and cook for 5 minutes to brown. Add the salt, pepper and rice and stir to combine. Add the cinnamon and nutmeg and stir again. Add the water, bring to the boil, then add the peas or broad beans and cook on a medium–low heat for 20 minutes, covered.

Meanwhile, in a separate pan, melt the butter, then cook the pine nuts until golden. Keep a close eye on them as they burn easily. Set aside.

Spoon the rice into serving dishes, add the buttered pine nuts, and serve alongside the yogurt dip.

Above: *Al-Nasira (Nazareth)*

Teta Najla's jazar mahshi

جزر محشي من ستّى نجلا

Traditional Gazan lamb-stuffed carrots

These carrots are tricky to make, but they work so well. Once I'd attempted them I called my mother and asked how on earth my little Teta made them as they are quite laborious, and she simply answered, 'Teta used to go to the electric shop and get them to drill them for her.' I nearly fell off my chair laughing, but I can see why she did. I do hope you will take the time to try them, as the sauce of tamarind with the mint and garlic is simply fantastic next to the slightly tangy and sweet carrots and the minced lamb and spices. Yum!

Serves 4–6

12–15 red/purple carrots
100g fresh tamarind in
    200ml warm water
juice of 1 lemon
1–2 tsp salt
5 garlic cloves, crushed
2 tsp olive oil
2 tsp dried mint
handful of fresh flat-leaf
    parsley, chopped, to
    serve

For the filling
100g Egyptian rice
100g lamb mince
20ml sunflower oil
½ tsp ground cinnamon
½ tsp cracked black pepper
1 tsp salt

Core your carrots carefully using an apple corer and a small butter knife to help scrape out the rest of the carrot once you have made an incision. This is going to take a while as they are quite hard and fragile. You will only be able to core them halfway, so work slowly. And wear gloves as they will stain.

For the filling, combine the rice with the lamb, oil and seasonings in a bowl.

Gently, without forcing, fill the carrots with the meat mixture, tapping the base of the carrot on your work surface to help it move down. You don't want to press the mixture in too deeply with your fingers, as it will not allow any of the juices to flow in to cook the meat and rice and you will be left with a raw mix.

Place the stuffed carrots into a wide-based pan and cover with the strained tamarind water, lemon juice and salt. Add enough water to cover the carrots to ensure they are all cooked properly and let them simmer over a medium heat for about 1 hour.

While the carrots are cooking, sauté the garlic in the olive oil until pinkish – don't let it go brown. Add the dried mint and stir through.

When the carrots are cooked through, drizzle most of this oil into the pot and leave the rest for drizzling over each serving plate.

The stock of the carrots should be a beautiful magenta colour. This is where the flavours are, so don't get rid of the sauce. Serve 2–3 carrots per person with a ladleful of sauce, a sprinkling of parsley and a drizzle of oil, and eat straight away.

Above: Al-Khalil (Hebron)

Teta Huda's silek mahshi

شيخ المحشي من ستي هدى

Swiss chard wrapped around minced lamb and rice

Palestinians love to stuff anything – literally anything – from carrots to courgettes to artichokes, to any leaf we can find, and these beautiful Swiss chard leaves are one of my favourites. They are cooked similarly to vine leaves, but for a much shorter time as the leaves are very soft. We don't add lemon to this dish as it makes the iron in the leaves really bitter, so it's just salted water and the spices in the meat mixture for flavouring. This takes time to prepare but is totally worth it. This recipe reminds me of my father's mother, Teta Huda, who was famous for her perfectly wrapped leaves. There is an old saying that the more perfect they are, the more you loved and appreciated the people you made them for, and we sure felt the love.

Serves 6–8

1kg fresh Swiss chard leaves, trimmed and washed (you will be left with about 650g)
300g lamb mince
100g Egyptian rice
2 tsp salt
2 tsp cracked black pepper
2 tsp ground cinnamon
2 tbsp olive oil
8 baby aubergines
10 lamb cutlets

Begin by blanching your chard leaves in boiling water, literally for 30 seconds to 1 minute, then let them drain and sit under cold water. If the leaves are big, you will want to cut them to half or a third of their size.

Combine the mince, rice, seasonings and olive oil in a bowl and mix well.

Place the leaves on a table and add a small amount of the rice and meat filling to the widest end of each one, where the stalk has been removed. You don't want to overfill them as the rice will swell and literally rip through the leaf. Fold the edges over the mixture and roll each one like a cigar, sealing the ends. Keep going until you have filled and rolled all the leaves.

Hollow out the aubergines using an apple corer, then use a knife to scrape out any remaining bits, although don't hollow them out too far. Use the remaining rice to stuff the aubergines.

Place the lamb cutlets in the base of a large pan, then layer some of the chard leaves on top. Add the aubergines around the edge of the pan, and finish with the remaining chard leaves. Cover with water and use a small plate to sit on top of the leaves in the pan to hold them in place; they need to be snug, or when they cook they will open up. Cook over a medium–low heat for about 35–40 minutes.

Drain off any excess water, then remove the small plate, place a larger platter over the pot and flip it over carefully. Serve with yogurt and enjoy. I do like to squeeze a little lemon juice on mine, but no one else does that in my family!

Kufta bil khudar

Lamb kufta baked with an assortment of vegetables

My whole family loves this dish – it is always showing up on our dinner table. It's so comforting and easy to pull together, and it makes quite a large quantity so is a great dish to share with a large group. The small amount of vinegar in the recipe is my mother's secret. It's a simple thing, but it really brings the dish together. We always eat this with radishes and scoop it up with bread – and the great news is that it tastes even better the next day.

Serves 6–8

For the vegetables

2 tbsp sunflower oil

2 onions, finely diced

4 courgettes, cut into 1cm cubes

2 large aubergines, peeled in alternate strips and cut into 1cm cubes

1 tsp salt

4 potatoes, peeled and cut into 1cm cubes

6 tomatoes, peeled and cut into small dice

1 tsp ground cinnamon

1 tsp cracked black pepper

2 tbsp red wine vinegar

2 tbsp tomato purée

400ml water

For the meat

500g lamb mince

1 onion, puréed

30g fresh flat-leaf parsley, puréed

2 tbsp sunflower oil

2 tsp salt

1 tsp black pepper

radishes and sliced green peppers, to serve

To prepare the vegetables, place the oil in a pan and add the diced onions to soften for a few minutes. Add the courgettes, aubergines and salt to the mix and cook to soften for about 10 minutes. Then add the potatoes, tomatoes, cinnamon, pepper, vinegar, tomato purée and water and mix. Leave to cook over a medium–low heat for about 40 minutes until softened and you have a thick-textured sauce. You may need to add a little more water during cooking if it's becoming too thick.

Preheat the oven to 180ºC Fan (200ºC/400ºF/Gas 6).

While the vegetables are cooking, make the meat mixture. Combine the mince with the ground onions and parsley, and add the oil to help you create the kufta without them getting stuck on your hands. Season with the salt and pepper. Use your hands to form the mixture into small shapes – I make mine the size and shape of Medjool dates: long, slender and a little plump, all at the same time. Place on a baking tray and cook them in the oven for about 10 minutes to seal.

Remove from the oven and transfer to a deep oven dish. Place the vegetables over the top of the meat and return to the oven, covered with foil, for a further 40 minutes. If you want the kufta to be crunchier, remove the foil after 20 minutes and leave uncovered for the last half of the cooking.

Serve with plenty of radishes and green peppers.

Lamia's fattet makdous

عاليفتة مكدوس من لمياء

Aubergine and minced lamb bake with tamarind and tomato sauce

Fatteh is one of those dishes that is eaten across all of the Middle East. It is made in so many different ways and with so many different ingredients, which is what makes it such a fabulous dish. *Fatteh* is basically any dish that has fried or toasted bread at the base, which then absorbs the liquid of the dish. There is *fattet hummus* and *fattet djaj* (both of which are in my first book), and many more options. I love all of them, but I think this one just beats them, as I love tamarind, which plays an important role in this dish, making it tangy and smooth at the same time.

Serves 6–8

2 thick *Khubez* (page 89), cut into 2cm diamond shapes
sunflower oil
3 aubergines, cut into thick 3cm chunks, with strips of skin removed to resemble zebra stripes
olive oil
300g lamb mince
1 tsp salt
1 tsp black pepper
1 tsp ground cinnamon
small bunch of fresh flat-leaf parsley, chopped, to garnish

For the yogurt mix
800g thick Greek yogurt
2 garlic cloves, minced
1 green chilli, minced
1 tsp salt

For the tomato tamarind sauce
2 onions, cut into half-moon slices
2 x 500g cartons of tomato passata
4–5 tbsp tamarind liquid
1 tsp salt

Begin by making the bread. Preheat the oven to 190ºC Fan (210ºC/425ºF/Gas 6–7). Place the bread pieces on a tray, drizzle some sunflower oil over the top and cook until golden and crunchy, about 10–12 minutes.

While they are cooking, make the yogurt mix. Place the yogurt, garlic and chilli in a bowl, add the salt and place in the fridge.

Next, make the tomato tamarind sauce. Sauté the onions in a little sunflower oil for about 15 minutes until golden, then add the passata, tamarind and salt and let it stew for about 30 minutes.

Place enough sunflower oil in a heavy pot to fry the aubergines. You want to cook them until they are golden or a little more than that. Once they are all cooked, set them aside.

Heat a little olive oil in a pan over a high heat and sauté the mince, salt, pepper and cinnamon for about 10 minutes until browned and cooked through.

Now for the layering part: place the bread at the bottom of a deep dish, add the yogurt mixture over the top, followed by the tomato mixture all over the yogurt to cover it. You don't want to mix it together – it doesn't matter if it gets a little swirled in, but try to layer it. Then add the fried aubergines, then the meat over the top, and scatter with fresh parsley. And serve. It is literally heaven, and you won't be able to stop eating it, especially the toasted bread at the bottom which has soaked up all the flavours.

Auntie Dunia's kufta bil warak ma' batata

كفتة بالورق مع بطاطا من خالتي دنيا

Lamb kufta-stuffed vine leaves with tomatoes and potatoes

When people ask me what meat we eat back home, the answer is usually lamb, because it is readily available and it is cheaper than beef. My publisher was astonished at how many different dishes we could make with lamb when I presented her with my first book, but I assure you as I did her that they all have a different flavour and really stand out on their own. Lamb mince goes a long way in Palestine, and we can make the most fabulous dishes from it. This is one of my favourites. The vine leaves add a touch of tartness and keep the meat really moist underneath the crunchy roasted potatoes with the tangy tomatoes. This whole dish screams Palestine and all its glory.

Serves 6–8

1 x 700g packet of vine
 leaves, rinsed and drained
900g lamb mince
3 large onions: 1 chopped,
 2 cut into half-moon
 slices
bunch of fresh flat-leaf
 parsley, chopped
2–3 tsp salt
2 tsp cracked black pepper
2–3 medium potatoes,
 peeled and cut into
 rounds
2–3 medium tomatoes, cut
 into rounds
200ml water

Preheat the oven to 180ºC Fan (200ºC/400ºF/Gas 6).

Blanch the vine leaves in boiling water for 5 minutes, then set aside to cool.

Combine the lamb mince with the chopped onions and parsley, salt and pepper. Use your hands to make the mixture into flat, round patties, about 5cm in diameter. Place each patty into a vine leaf (or you may need to use two leaves per patty) and fold over to close and seal.

Parboil the potatoes for 7–8 minutes and set aside.

Scatter the half-moon onion slices over the base of a 30cm baking dish. Place the sealed meat patties on top, followed by the tomatoes and finishing with a layer of potatoes.

Pour the water into the base of the dish, cover with foil and bake for 70 minutes. Increase the oven temperature to 200ºC Fan (220ºC/ 425ºF/Gas 7), remove the foil and bake for a further 25 minutes until the potatoes are golden in colour.

Ma'carona bil lahmeh

معكرونة باللحمة

Macaroni with tangy yogurt and spiced lamb mince

I thought my mum had made this dish up when I first tried it, but she assured me that it was served by her mother for her eleven children. It is a quicker version of *Shishbarak* (page 105), and was served during the winter months in El-Lydd, but I serve it all year round because it's just delicious.

Serves 4–6

500g macaroni
700g Greek yogurt
juice of 1 lemon
1 green chilli, finely
  chopped
2 garlic cloves, minced
2 tsp salt
75ml olive oil
500g lamb mince
1 tsp black pepper
1 tsp ground cinnamon
50–75g toasted pine nuts
small bunch of fresh flat-
  leaf parsley, chopped

Bring a large pan of salted water to the boil and cook the pasta according to the packet instructions.

Combine the yogurt with the lemon juice, chilli, garlic and 1 teaspoon of salt in a bowl, and place in the fridge.

Heat the oil in a frying pan over a high heat, and sauté the lamb mince with the pepper, cinnamon and remaining salt for 12–15 minutes until browned and cooked through, then set aside.

When the pasta has finished cooking, drain and place in a large bowl. Take the yogurt mix from the fridge and mix it through the pasta, then add the lamb mixture on top, but don't mix it in. Scatter the pine nuts and chopped parsley on top and serve. It is so delicious and simple, but tastes like home for me.

Aqaba Village, Tubas

Kastaleta bil za'atar wa dibs rumman

كستاليتا بالزعتر و دبس الرمان

Pomegranate and za'atar lamb chops with lemon, mint and yogurt

This dish – of lamb, pomegranates and za'atar – really is the essence of home. I loved it so much when I was putting it together that I couldn't leave it out, as it is simply delicious, with the taste of Palestine running through it. The yogurt adds a tangy freshness to the lamb when eaten together.

Serves 4

12 lamb chops, kept in
    sections of 3, French
    trimmed (ask your
    butcher)
2 tbsp sunflower oil
3–4 tbsp pomegranate
    molasses
2 tsp za'atar
1 tsp chilli flakes
1 tsp salt
handful of pomegranate
    seeds

For the yogurt mix
250g Greek yogurt
grated zest and juice of
    1 lemon
pinch of dried mint
1 garlic clove, grated
pinch of salt
olive oil, to drizzle

Preheat the oven to 190ºC Fan (210ºC/425ºF/Gas 6–7).

Sear the lamb racks in the oil in a hot pan to render down some fat. This will help colour the meat as well. Once they have taken on a little colour, place them on a baking tray and rub them with the pomegranate molasses, za'atar and chilli and season with salt. Make sure the rub is all over the lamb so it is evenly flavoured.

Place in the hot oven and cook for a further 10–12 minutes, depending on how well done you like your meat. You can cook it for longer if you want it more well done, but I like mine pink.

While the lamb is cooking, combine all the yogurt ingredients in a bowl, mixing well, then spread over the base of your serving dish and drizzle with olive oil.

Remove the lamb from the oven, cut into chops and place on top of the yogurt. Scatter over a handful of pomegranate seeds and serve with a dollop of the yogurt. Alternatively, serve each person a section of three chops, which they cut away from each other to reveal the inside of the meat.

Al-Mughayyir, Jenin

Fayza's idreh / Ruz madfoun

قدرة فايرة / رز مدفون

Spiced rice and lamb with chickpeas and toasted nuts

It's always a hot topic when discussing where certain dishes come from, and this is even true within Palestine itself. This dish is cooked all over the country, but it is typically known in Al-Khalil (Hebron), where it is cooked differently to the way my mother showed me (she is from El-Lydd). My friend Khaled also introduced me to this dish, and his mother showed me the Gazan way of making it. In Al-Khalil they don't use the garlic, and in many cases they don't add the chickpeas – but I am going with my mum and Auntie Fayza's recipe. It's a winner for me. *Idreh* is traditionally cooked in a special clay pot. It is so beautifully spiced and hearty that it makes a fantastic and relatively cheap meal.

Serves 8–10

For the lamb

3.5 litres water

2kg lamb shoulder, cut into 2cm cubes

3 onions, quartered

10 cardamom pods

2 cinnamon sticks

2 tsp salt

For the rice

2 onions, diced

150ml sunflower oil

4 whole heads of garlic, cloves removed but skin on

240g tinned chickpeas, drained

4 tsp ground turmeric

1 tsp ground cinnamon

1 tsp ground cardamom

1 tsp black pepper

1–2 tsp salt

500g basmati rice, plus 1 tbsp ground turmeric

toasted pine nuts and almonds, to scatter

fresh flat-leaf parsley, to scatter

Greek yogurt, to serve

In a large lidded pan, boil the water with the lamb, onions, cardamom pods, cinnamon sticks and salt for a minimum of 1 hour.

While the meat is cooking, sauté the diced onions in the sunflower oil over a medium heat. Add the garlic cloves and mix until softened. Add a splash of water to soften further, then add the chickpeas and all the spices and salt.

Wash the rice and add the turmeric to colour it, then add this to the onions and spices and toss until fully coated in all the flavours.

Drain the lamb, reserving the meat and stock and discarding the onions, cardamom and cinnamon sticks. Add the cooked meat to the rice and toss all the ingredients together. Add enough of the reserved stock to cover up to a knuckle's worth over the rice; top up with water if necessary.

Cover and cook over a low heat for about 30 minutes, until the rice is cooked through. Once it is ready, turn out onto a large serving platter and scatter with the toasted nuts and parsley leaves. Alternatively, you can serve straight from the pot, and always with Greek yogurt – it's a must.

Shahrazade's mansaf

منسف شهرازاد

Traditional turmeric rice with lamb

Mansaf is a dish that is traditionally eaten in Palestine, although in recent years it has become more associated with Jordan as their national dish. Of course our close proximity tends to mean that food does cross the border, but this is not a matter of who the dish belongs to, rather that it is enjoyed by both countries. *Mansaf* is usually eaten around a large table, and usually by hand as Bedouins used to do. It has the most wonderful sour taste as it is made with dried yogurt and then mixed with lamb stock and served over a golden rice of turmeric. Make this when you have friends over – it is a great dish to be enjoyed by the many.

Serves 10–12

2.2kg lamb shoulder, bone in, cut into 12 pieces
10 cardamom pods
20 black peppercorns
2 bay leaves
1 tbsp salt
2 onions, quartered
3.5 litres water
240g jameed (dried yogurt)
500g Greek yogurt
50g butter
150g almonds
150g pine nuts
1 x shop-bought saj bread (or similar flatbread)
fresh flat-leaf parsley, chopped, to scatter

For the rice

100ml sunflower oil
10 cardamom pods
500g Egyptian rice
500g basmati rice
1 level tbsp salt
2 tsp ground turmeric
1.5 litres water

Place the lamb cuts into a pan of boiling water and bring to the boil for about 10 minutes, then discard the water to get rid of any scum.

Return the lamb to the pan with all the seasonings, onions and the 3.5 litres of water and cook over a medium–low heat for about 2 hours. You want the lamb to be falling off the bone. Keep checking the water does not evaporate fully during cooking. You will need some stock to finish the dish. While the meat is cooking, soak the jameed in hot water, just enough to cover it, so it breaks down and becomes easier to work with.

Prepare the rice. Heat the sunflower oil in a pan, add the cardamom pods to flavour, then add the rice. Mix well and add the salt. Add the turmeric and the water and mix well to colour and flavour the rice, then cook on a medium–low heat for about 20–25 minutes with a lid on.

Add the Greek yogurt to the jameed in a bowl and mix together.

When the lamb has finished cooking, add 1.2 litres of strained stock to the yogurt mixture and combine well. You may have to use a blender to get a silky smooth texture; you don't want any lumps. Once you reach the desired consistency, transfer to a pan, add the lamb to the mixture and cook on the hob over a medium–low heat for about 30 minutes.

Heat the butter in a frying pan and brown off the nuts for a few minutes.

Place the bread on a large serving platter. Spoon the rice on top and place the lamb pieces on the bed of rice. Drizzle over the yogurt, then scatter over the parsley and buttered nuts and serve.

Lahem mahshi bil ruz

لحم محشي بالرز

Stuffed lamb shoulder

Stuffed lamb shoulder is one of the greats. This is truly a celebration of the mighty lamb, as not only are we cooking the lamb shoulder, we are also stuffing it with minced lamb and rice seasoned perfectly with cinnamon and nutmeg. This is a festive dish, very important to us during the time of Ramadan and especially Eid. The meat falls off the bone and is so delicate. You can also scatter it with some buttered pine nuts and almonds to make it even more of a showstopper.

Serves 4–6

1.5kg shoulder of lamb, deboned but with the top bone in
1 bay leaf
2 cardamom pods
1 cinnamon stick
2–3 cloves
500ml water

For the marinade

1 tsp cracked black pepper
½ tsp ground cinnamon
½ tsp grated nutmeg
1 tsp salt
½ tsp ground cardamom powder

For the stuffing

4 tbsp sunflower oil
500g lamb mince
2 tsp grated nutmeg
2 tsp ground cinnamon
1 tsp cracked black pepper
2 tsp salt
360g Egyptian rice

Combine all the marinade ingredients together in a bowl and rub all over the meat. Set aside to marinate for 30 minutes.

For the stuffing, heat the oil in a pan over a high heat and sauté the mince, spices and salt for 10–12 minutes. Add the rice, cover with water by 2cm, and cook for 10–12 minutes over a medium–low heat, with the lid on. Remove one-third of the part-cooked rice and use it to stuff the lamb shoulder, stitching the lamb with cooking twine to encase the stuffing. Leave the remaining rice to cook for another 10 minutes, then set aside. Preheat the oven to 190ºC Fan (210ºC/425ºF/Gas 6–7).

Sear the lamb in a hot pan for a few minutes, then transfer it to a roasting tray with the bay leaf, cardamom, cinnamon, cloves and water, with the side to be presented when serving placed face-down in the tray. Cover in foil and cook for 2 hours.

When you are ready to serve, re-heat the remaining rice in a pan, low oven or microwave for a few minutes. Sit the lamb on the bed of rice and slice.

Right: Jenin

From left to right: Shawermat djaj aw lahmeh

Shawermat djaj aw lahmeh

شاورمة دجاج أولحمة

Chicken or beef shawerma with pickled turnips and cucumbers

Serves 8–10

1kg chicken breast, cut into
long, thin slices
OR
1kg lean beef, preferably
fillet or sirloin, cut into
long, thin slices
6–8 tbsp sunflower oil
shop-bought flatbreads, to
serve
pickled turnips, pickled
cucumbers, pickled
chillies, and sliced onions
mixed with sumac and
fresh parsley, to serve

For the spice rub
1 tbsp ground coriander
1 tbsp ground cumin
1½ tbsp garlic powder
1 tsp cracked black pepper
1 tsp allspice
1 tsp ground ginger
1 tsp ground cloves
1 tsp paprika
1¼ tsp ground turmeric
1 tsp ground cinnamon
1–2 tsp salt

For the marinade
1 red onion, thinly sliced
10 garlic cloves, chopped
100ml red wine vinegar
120ml white wine vinegar
75ml olive oil

For the tahini sauce
4 tbsp tahini
6 tbsp Greek yogurt
juice of 2 lemons
1–2 tsp salt

Who doesn't like shawerma? It is a staple of Palestine, especially popular at markets and restaurants. I adore it – as long as it's done right. This is made with a medley of spices and marinades that really do make this dish. The pickles are a must, too. I have made a big batch here as it is a shame to make only a couple of sandwiches – trust me, you won't have any leftovers.

Combine all the ingredients for the spice rub together in a bowl. In a separate bowl, combine all the marinade ingredients.

Place the chicken or beef in a bowl. Rub the spice mixture all over the meat, then pour over the marinade and leave to marinate for at least 6 hours, or ideally overnight (it is fine to marinate for up to 3 days in the fridge).

For the tahini sauce, combine all the ingredients in a bowl and leave in the fridge. You will have to water it down a little before using as it will have thickened up.

Once the meat has marinated, place the oil in a pan over a medium-high heat. Add the chicken or beef to the hot pan and cook until the meat is cooked through, about 5–6 minutes. Do this in batches so it doesn't overcrowd the pan.

When the meat is ready you can make your wrap: spread the tahini sauce over a flatbread and top with your choice of pickles and onions, then add your meat and fold it over like a burrito.

*Djaj bil za'faran
wal zaytoun*

Djaj bil za'faran wal zaytoun

دجاج بالزعفران والزيتون

Saffron chicken with preserved lemon and pilaf rice

This dish is definitely not from Palestine (I am sure there is a North African influence somewhere in there), but it appeared on our dinner table quite often. We love preserved lemons and olives, and of course chicken too. My mum had plenty of us to feed, yet she never cooked the same thing twice for weeks at a time, something I truly admire – she loved variety and wanted us to experience lots of different foods.

Serves 4

For the chicken
50g butter
2 onions, finely diced
5 cardamom pods
1 bay leaf
pinch of saffron
1 tsp salt
100g unpitted Teta Huda's
    Zaytoun (page 206), or
    use green olives from a
    Middle Eastern specialist
    supermarket
1 tsp tomato purée
1 whole chicken, cut into 4
    or 6 pieces with bones
2 preserved lemons, cut
    into wedges

For the rice
50g butter
2 tbsp olive oil
2 onions, finely diced
5 cardamom pods, crushed
1 tsp salt
300g basmati rice

fresh flat-leaf parsley,
    chopped, to garnish

For the chicken, melt the butter in a large deep pan, add the onions and let them caramelize slightly for about 10 minutes.

Add the cardamom pods, bay leaf, saffron and salt and cook off for about 1–2 minutes. Add the olives and tomato purée and stir through. Now add the chicken pieces and mix everything thoroughly. Finally, add the preserved lemon wedges, cover the chicken with water and cook for a further 35–40 minutes. Keep checking that the water has not disappeared; you want some liquid there, as this should not be dry. Check the liquid for flavour, and if it needs more salt add it now so it can flavour the chicken well.

While the chicken is cooking, prepare the rice. Place the butter and olive oil in a pan and sauté the onions until brown. Add the cardamom pods, salt and rice and mix to combine. Add enough water to cover the rice by a knuckle's worth, place the lid on the pan and cook on a medium–low heat for about 20 minutes.

Serve each person a portion of rice and place a piece of the delicious amber chicken over it. Garnish with some chopped parsley.

Chicken à la Mo

دجاج على طريقة اخي مو

Mo is my brother, and cooking did not pass him by as we were growing up – everyone was involved in our house. My dad was the king of the Palestinian barbecue, so it is only natural that my brother has the cooking gene in him. This dish came about when my parents were away and we had eaten our way through all the prepared frozen meals and were left with literally chicken and little else. Even though we were hungry, we knew we still had to eat something amazing! So this happened. Some people will say it is not Palestinian, but even if my mum cooked a pizza it would be a Palestinian pizza.

Serves 4

1.3kg whole chicken

2 Pink Lady apples, peeled and cut into chunks

3 carrots, peeled and cut into chunks

2 onions, quartered,

2 red or green chillies, sliced halfway

2 whole heads of garlic, cloves separated and skin on

4–5 sprigs of fresh thyme leaves

200g baby potatoes, skin on

2 tbsp olive oil

750ml water

salt and freshly ground black pepper

Preheat the oven to 190ºC Fan (210ºC/425ºF/Gas 6–7).

Season the chicken with salt and pepper, then place the chicken, breast side down, in a roasting tray. In a bowl, combine all the remaining ingredients, except the water, then add this to the roasting tray. I like to place some of the mixture in the cavity of the chicken and then lay the rest around it. Add the water.

Transfer to the oven for 40 minutes, then turn and cook breast side up for a further 40 minutes, or until golden. Remove and serve with the accompanying vegetables. The liquid will have turned into a wonderful gravy, with all the fabulous flavours of the vegetables, chilli, garlic and apples.

Right: Ein Hamed, Al-Quds (Jerusalem)

Djaj mahshi bil freekeh

دجاج محشي بالفريكة

Poussin stuffed with green-herbed freekeh

Freekeh is literally one of the best grains out there. It is green and nutty and has this amazing aroma when cooked. It is also now rated as one of the healthiest things you can eat, so this dish is definitely good for you. Palestinians love adding spices and herbs to food, especially nearer the coastal areas where they are in abundance. Freekeh is used in many stuffings, as it is filling and hearty, and it works really well with chicken, or I prefer poussin. The herbs literally burst with flavour in your mouth.

Serves 6

300g freekeh

100g fresh flat-leaf parsley, chopped

50g fresh chives, chopped

bunch of fresh mint, chopped

170g fresh coriander, chopped

4 spring onions, chopped

2 garlic cloves, minced

1 tsp salt

1 tsp cracked black pepper

1 tsp crushed red chillies

grated zest and juice of 1 lemon

50ml olive oil, plus extra to drizzle

6 poussin

1 x quantity Yogurt Dip (page 178), to serve

Preheat the oven to 180°C Fan (200°C/400°F/Gas 6).

Combine all the ingredients, except the poussin, together in a bowl and check for flavour. Place the mixture into the cavity of the poussin and place them in a deep baking dish.

Season the poussin with some extra salt and pepper and a drizzle of olive oil, and add water to the dish so the lower half of the poussin is submerged. Cover with foil and cook for about 1 hour. The water will flavour from the chicken, herbs and freekeh and will create a delicious sauce once it's ready.

Once cooked, ladle some sauce over the poussin and serve one for each person, with a little yogurt dip alongside.

Right: *Ein Karem, Al-Quds (Jerusalem)*

Firri mashwi ma' salatet dagga

فرّي مشوي مع سلطة دقة

Marinated and roasted quail with a spicy tomato sauce

When we were young we used to go to an Arabic restaurant on Sundays, as we would always have friends and other family with us and my mum would take a break from cooking. I remember very clearly that I used to love the marinated quail, and it was just such a treat as we never really ate them at home (although my mum is the best at making them). This recipe for roasted spatchcock quail is simple and deserves to be the highlight of the table, especially with the spicy *dagga* sauce that is most popular in Gaza.

Serves 4

4 quail, spatchcocked
4 garlic cloves, smashed
handful of fresh flat-leaf
　parsley, chopped
handful of fresh dill,
　chopped
1 tsp chilli flakes
juice and grated zest of 1
　lemon
2 tbsp olive oil
salt

For the spicy tomato
　sauce
2–3 garlic cloves
2 red hot chillies, chopped
4 ripened plum tomatoes,
　chopped
10g fresh dill
juice of ½ lemon
50ml olive oil

Preheat the oven to 200ºC Fan (220ºC/425ºF/Gas 7). Place the spatchcocked quail breast side down on a baking tray.

Put the garlic, parsley, dill, chilli flakes and lemon juice and zest into a bowl, season with the olive oil and salt, and mix to combine.

Put half the mixture onto the quail and place the quail in the oven for about 10 minutes, then turn them over. Add the rest of the spice mixture on top of the quail and cook for a further 25 minutes.

To make the sauce, please try and use a pestle and mortar. This is how we make it back home and it just releases the flavours better. If you do have to use a blender, then pulse, don't pulverize.

Begin by grinding the garlic cloves, then add the chillies and release the flavours. Add the tomatoes and the dill and grind away. You don't want to create a purée, but you do want the ingredients to blend together. Add the lemon juice and salt to taste, and once you are happy with the taste and consistency, add the oil.

Place the quail on a platter and drizzle over the sauce – the finished dish always looks so beautiful.

From the River to the Sea

FISH

Along the coast of Palestine, in cities and towns such as Haifa, Yaffa and Gaza, you will come across some beautiful fish dishes. The coast is vibrant and fresh, although fishing is a little more restricted than in the time of my Tetas, so fishermen today have to make do with a smaller catch and less variety. This chapter includes some very traditional recipes, while others I have created with the essence of Palestine due to our somewhat limited repertoire in this area.

Dishes like *Samakeh Harra* (page 171), *Samak Makli* (page 178) and *Kubbet Samak* (page 180) show how people from different regions of Palestine cook their fish, according to the climate and the produce they have available. Eating in Palestine is organic – it makes the most of the natural placement of foods that connect with each other well and can be used in harmony with each other. Putting dishes together using local ingredients, combining different flavours, is what makes our cuisine so natural, free and vibrant. You just know that something will taste good if you combine the right elements together.

Here you will find food bursting with chilli, lemon, garlic and plenty of herbs, such as dill and *dagga* sauces. You can be as free as you want and change things up as you prefer, but spice is the main element in this part of the country and really brings the recipes alive. I hope you enjoy these dishes, as they are very much reminiscent of my grandmothers and their mothers before them, and the beautiful shores of Palestine.

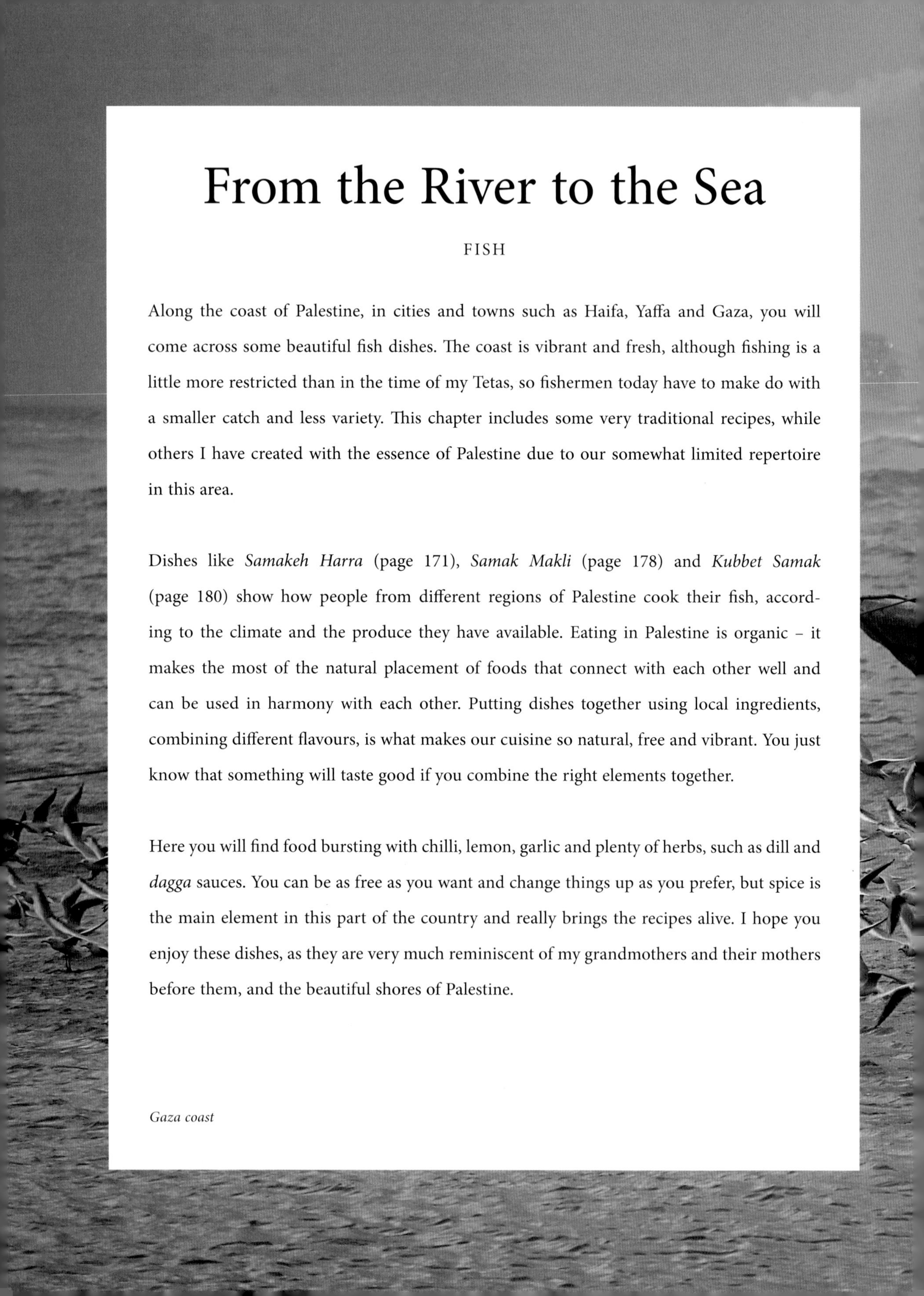

Gaza coast

All images: Gaza Seaport

Salamoun bil arak

Salamoun bil arak

سلمون بالعرق

Arak-poached salmon

Salmon is not typically used back home, but seeing as it is readily accessible, this recipe works well with the fattiness of the fish. I made this for a client who loves Middle Eastern food but wanted to use salmon instead of white fish, and it worked beautifully. The arak and lemon against the fatty fish is perfect, and the dill really brings out the flavour of it all.

Serves 6–8

1 tbsp English mustard
75g fresh dill, roughly
    chopped
4 tbsp arak
juice of 2 lemons
2 tsp pink peppercorns
1 whole side skinless
    salmon fillet, approx.
    900g

For the rice
50g butter, melted
1 onion, diced
2 tsp coriander seeds
grated zest of 1 lemon
1 tsp salt
200g basmati rice

Combine the mustard, dill, arak, lemon juice and peppercorns in a bowl. Add the fish and leave to marinate for about 20 minutes in the fridge before slicing into 6–8 pieces.

Preheat the oven to 200ºC Fan (220ºC/425ºF/Gas 7). Prepare the rice by melting the butter in a frying pan and caramelizing the onions for about 10–12 minutes. Add the coriander seeds, lemon zest, salt and rice and mix well. Add enough water to cover by a knuckle's worth, and cook over a medium heat for about 15–20 minutes.

While the rice is cooking, place the salmon pieces in a small baking tray and cover with water, then place in the oven and cook for about 12–15 minutes, depending on how pink you like your fish. You can cook it for longer if you like.

When the rice and fish have finished cooking, place a portion of rice on to each serving plate and serve one piece of salmon per person.

Below: *View from old town of Yaffa*

Sardines manou' bil zeit wa laymoun wa harr

سمك السردين المنقوع بالزيت والليمون والحر

Marinated sardines

My mother's family, who lived by the sea, ate so many amazing dishes that my father's family, in the north, had never even heard of. It is incredible that within such a small country, people had such different experiences with food. My Teta didn't eat raw fish, but lightly grilled it. My mother is more adventurous and marinates fish in lemon and other flavours, which partially cook the flesh. This is a modern version of Teta's classic – like her, you can grill the sardines for about 2 minutes if you wish.

Serves 4

8–12 sardines, filleted
1 garlic clove, crushed
1 red chilli, crushed
small bunch of fresh flat-
    leaf parsley, chopped
2 tsp white wine vinegar
4 tbsp olive oil
juice of 1 lemon
1 spring onion, chopped
2 tomatoes, cubed

For the salad
150g maftoul
2 tsp salt
30g fresh dill, chopped
30g fresh flat-leaf parsley,
    chopped
1 red chilli, chopped
2 tomatoes, diced
2 spring onions, diced
50–75ml olive oil
juice of 2 lemons
1 tsp salt

Place the sardines on a flat platter and add the remaining ingredients. Mix well and leave in the fridge to marinate for at least 1 hour.

Meanwhile, bring a pan of water to the boil and add the maftoul and salt. Cook until al dente, approximately 12–15 minutes, but please keep checking as all maftoul types are different and some may need less time and others more. These are handmade balls so they are never equal sizes.

Once cooked, drain the maftoul and add the remaining ingredients; these will reflect what is in the marinade for the sardines. Check the seasoning and place the salad in a serving platter. Serve the sardines on top or plate up individually.

Right: Gaza

Luqus bil shatta al-khadra

لقس بالشطة الخضراء

Green shatta-marinated sea bass with crushed dried rose petals

I like to use shatta on pretty much everything – it is like the Sriracha of the Middle East, just better! Shatta is always best made by hand in a pestle and mortar, as grinding it this way will give you the right consistency. It should be chunky and smooth all at the same time, with plenty of flavour. Shatta is usually made using red chillies, but I love both red and green, and this is a green version; the method is the same for both, but they each have a different heat. I love using this on fish as it complements it well. Shatta and fish are traditionally eaten by the coast, and this is very much a Gazan delicacy.

Serves 4

1 x 1.5kg sea bass, scaled and gutted

1 tsp salt

½ lemon, cut into half-moon slices (cook the remaining half with the fish)

¼ x quantity green Shatta (page 42)

dried, crushed rose petals, to serve

Preheat the oven to 180ºC Fan (200ºC/400ºF/Gas 6). Place the fish on a piece of baking parchment inside a baking dish and make three cuts into the scales on each side of the fish, then sprinkle the top and insides with salt. Add the lemon moons into the incisions that you have made, then place some of the shatta inside and on top of the fish, along with the remaining half lemon.

Place in the oven for 40–45 minutes until the eyes of the fish are opaque and the fish has a slightly charred effect to it.

Remove from the oven and drizzle with the remaining shatta. Scatter some dried rose petals over the top. Not only does the colour of the roses look fabulous against the green of the sauce, but the taste is really delicate, creating a lovely balance of flavours.

Shahla's samakeh harrah

سمكة حرة بالطحينة من خالتي شهلا

Spicy fish in a tahini, yogurt, lemon and parsley sauce

Samakeh harra is one of my all-time favourite dishes. I have a similar recipe to this in my first book, *Palestine on a Plate*, which is the version that my mother's family use. They are from the coastal area of Palestine, from El-Lydd and Yaffa, which means theirs is lighter and sharper. My father's family is from Safad, which is closer to the border of Lebanon, so they are in the north of Palestine where the climate is colder, and this is reflected in the slightly heavier dishes that they make. This version is cooked with tahini sauce and cayenne pepper and covered with toasted pine nuts. I like to eat this with rice to make it more of a meal. Simply heavenly.

Serves 2–4

1 x 800g white fish of your choice (I use sea bream), scaled and gutted
1 tsp salt
juice of 1 lemon
200g pine nuts
50g butter, melted
pinch of paprika
small handful of fresh flat-leaf parsley, roughly chopped
olive oil, to drizzle

For the tahini sauce
6 tbsp Greek yogurt
3 tbsp tahini
juice of 2–3 lemons
1 tsp cayenne pepper
100ml water
salt, to taste (it all really depends on what kind of tahini you use)

Preheat the oven to 180ºC Fan (200ºC/400ºF/Gas 6). Place the fish in a baking dish on baking parchment or kitchen foil, season with the salt and lemon juice and cook for 30–40 minutes until the eyes become opaque and the flesh tender.

While the fish is cooking, prepare the sauce by combining all the ingredients in a bowl. It should not be too thin as it won't hold on to the fish while it cooks for the last 10 minutes, which is what you want it to do. Taste the sauce for seasoning – it should be tangy, creamy and spicy. Add more salt if necessary, and when you are happy with the flavour, set it aside.

In a pan, toast the pine nuts in the butter until golden brown; don't cook them for any longer than this as they can become quite bitter.

Remove the fish from the oven, then remove the baking parchment from underneath the fish and discard. Drizzle the tahini sauce over the fish, reserving just a little for serving. Place it back in the oven for a further 10 minutes to cook and heat through. My mother likes to remove the bones from the fish before she adds the sauce, and then place the fillets back over each other again, but this is all a bit messy for me, so I like to keep it whole and let people do it for themselves.

Once the fish is cooked, warm the remaining tahini sauce in a pan and pour it over the fish. Scatter over the pine nuts, paprika and parsley, drizzle with olive oil and serve straight away.

Above: Coast at Haifa

Sultan Ibrahim bil shatta al-khadra

سلطان ابراهيم بالشطة الخضراء

Green shatta-marinated red mullet with pickled red onions on pita bread

Sultan Ibrahim (red mullet) is one of the most iconic fish in the Middle East. The pink- and gold-flecked skin and the tender sweet flesh is so beautiful, and is eaten very simply with a little seasoning and a squeeze of lemon. Inspired by Gaza's hot spicy shatta, I decided to make this in a way that I like to eat, and I have to say it turned out great. I ate it for breakfast– yes, I am that girl who eats garlicky chilli sauce with fish for breakfast – but it's wonderful at any time of day, of course.

Serves 3–4

8 red mullet fillets

juice of 2 lemons

1 x quantity green Shatta (page 42)

1 red onion, cut into half-moon slices

2 tbsp red wine vinegar

1 tsp caster sugar

1 tsp sumac

2 tbsp olive oil

small bunch of fresh flat-leaf parsley, chopped

juice of ½ lemon

pinch of salt

3–4 shop-bought flatbreads

In a large bowl, marinate the red mullet fillets in the lemon juice and shatta for 2 hours (or up to 24 hours) in the fridge.

Toss all the remaining ingredients, except the flatbreads, together in a bowl and set aside.

Place the flatbreads on a plate and scatter the salad over the top. Top with 2–3 fillets, wrap up and eat straight away.

Salamoun bi dibs al-rumman

سالمون بصلصة دبس الرمان

Salmon skewers with pomegranate marinade

Salmon is not common in the waters of the Middle East, so it is not really a fish that we eat, but it is delicious and there is no reason why we can't use it here with influences of home. I like to try many different things while cooking, and always look for ways to create flavours that are familiar. I made this a lot in my deli, Baity Kitchen, and it was very well received. It is delicate, and the sourness of the marinade against the fatty salmon works wonderfully.

Serves 2–4

You will need:
2–4 metal skewers

500g skinless salmon fillet,
    cut into 2.5cm slices
2 tbsp sunflower oil

For the marinade
5 tbsp pomegranate
    molasses
2 tbsp honey
pinch of chilli flakes (you
    can add more if you like)
1 tsp salt
juice of ½ lemon
50ml olive oil

For the salad
1 onion, cut into half-moon
    slices
50g rocket
3 small preserved lemons,
    cut into thin wedges
1½ tsp sumac
25g fresh flat-leaf parsley
1 tsp salt
1 tbsp olive oil

Place all the marinade ingredients into a bowl with the salmon and leave to marinate in the fridge for 20–30 minutes.

Combine all the salad ingredients and set aside.

When the salmon is ready, place a non-stick pan over a medium–low heat and add the oil. Place the salmon in the pan, flesh side down, and don't move for 2–3 minutes, then turn over with a spatula and cook the other side. You can add the remaining marinade while it is cooking, but be careful it doesn't burn as there is a high sugar content in the honey and pomegranate molasses.

Once you are happy with the salmon – I like mine slightly pink inside, but you can cook it for longer if you like – place the salad on to a plate, thread the salmon pieces onto skewers and serve alongside the salad. I skewer the pieces after cooking, as it is easier to cook them in a pan, but if you have a flat grill please skewer them first. I just think it makes for a nicer presentation.

Right: *Sea at Yaffa*

Samak abyad bil z'afaran

سمك ابيض بالزعفران

Saffron monkfish and vegetable skewers

We eat a lot of white fish in Palestine, as it is readily available. Monkfish is not a fish we usually eat, but I'm using it here as it has a meaty texture that holds its shape really well and is easy to cook. It takes slightly longer to cook than most white fish as it is a little more dense.

Serves 2–4

You will need:
2–4 metal skewers

pinch of saffron
2 monkfish tails, deboned
   and cut into 8 long slices
   (each monkfish will give
   you 2 fillets, so cut them
   again to get 4 from each
   fish)
1 tbsp honey
juice of 1 lemon
1 courgette, cut into rings
1 red pepper, roughly
   chopped
1 tbsp sunflower oil
50g lamb's lettuce
½ onion, cut into half-moon
   slices
pinch of sumac
olive oil
salt
lemon wedges, to serve
   (optional)

Place the saffron in a bowl and add 5 tablespoons of hot water to release the flavour. If you want a more intense flavour, add more saffron, but do be careful as it can overpower everything. Add the fillets to the bowl with the honey, half the lemon juice, all the vegetables and a pinch of salt. Transfer to the fridge to marinate for 10 minutes to create the flavour you require.

Place the pieces of fish on skewers with the vegetables; use one or two fish per skewer, depending on the size. Each skewer should only have a little of the vegetables and fish on it.

Heat the sunflower oil in a flat griddle pan over a low heat and cook the fish gently. You want it to cook for a while, about 10 minutes, as it is meaty and a little bit tough if undercooked. It should be slightly flaky. Remove the fish from the pan and set aside.

Toss the lamb's lettuce with the onion, sumac, the remaining lemon juice and a pinch of salt, and place on a serving platter with the fish on top. Drizzle over a little olive oil, and serve with some lemon wedges, if you like.

Samak makli bil camun

سمك مقلي بالكمون

Fried fish selection with courgette, mint and yogurt dip

This dish used to come out when there were many of us gathered together for dinner. We absolutely loved it and waited with bated breath for it to arrive at the table. My Mama would make so many different varieties of fish that everyone would be happy, and for me it's the perfect platter for when guests arrive. This is a reflection of her upbringing and my Teta Najla's life on the coast of Palestine.

Serves 4–6

juice and grated zest of 2 lemons
1 tsp ground cumin
1 tbsp cumin seeds
50ml olive oil
½ tsp black pepper
50g whitebait
8 small red mullet
250g salmon, cut into 5cm lengths
6 sardines, gutted and cleaned
1 squid, cut into rings
8 prawns, shells removed, heads and tails intact
sunflower oil, for frying
300g plain flour, seasoned with salt
small bunch of fresh flat-leaf parsley, to scatter
lemon wedges, to serve
salt

For the yogurt dip
400g Greek yogurt
1 courgette, grated
1 garlic clove, crushed
1 tsp salt
1–2 tsp dried mint

Combine the lemon juice and zest, ground cumin and seeds, olive oil, 1 teaspoon of salt and the pepper in a bowl, add all the fish and leave to marinate for about 30 minutes to an hour.

While the fish are marinating, combine all the ingredients for the yogurt dip in a bowl and set aside in the fridge.

Half-fill a deep pan with sunflower oil and heat it to 180ºC. Remove the fish from the marinade on to kitchen towel, then coat each piece in the seasoned flour. Dust off any excess flour and quickly fry them until they begin to turn slightly golden – literally only 1 minute for most of the pieces. Remember the marinade will have already started the cooking process, due to the lemon. Don't overcrowd the pan or it will take much longer to cook everything. When they are all cooked through – you will need to use your judgement as each piece is different in size to the next – sprinkle with salt and fresh parsley, and serve on a big platter with the dip and some lemon wedges, and off you go. It really is a taste of Teta's home.

Right: *Gaza Seaport*

Auntie Nuha's kubbet samak

كبة سمك على طريقة خالتي نهى

Mixed fried fish

Kubbeh is made in so many different ways – Syria is famous for kubbeh, and I think my Auntie Nuha, who spent part of her life there, brought those influences home with her. This is a fish kubbeh that is delicate and fresh due to the lemon and orange zest. I particularly love it with the tahini sauce.

Serves 6–8

For the filling

4 onions, sliced

50ml sunflower oil

1 tbsp salt

1 tbsp pepper

½ tsp ground cinnamon

½ tsp ground cumin

200g potted prawns

olive oil, to drizzle

For the topping and base

500g medium coarse
  bulgur wheat

1kg cod fillet, skinned and
  boned

1 tsp plain flour

1 tsp salt

1 tsp ground cumin

1 tsp ground cinnamon

1 tsp dried marjoram

1 tsp ground coriander

½ tsp black pepper

1 green chilli, chopped

4 sprigs of fresh mint,
  finely chopped

15g fresh coriander, finely
  chopped

grated zest of ½ lemon

grated zest of ½ orange

1 onion, finely grated

1 x quantity Tahini Sauce
  (omit the cayenne pepper
  – page 171)

For the filling, sauté the onions in the oil for about 10 minutes until softened and slightly caramelized. Add the salt, spices and prawns and mix for a couple more minutes. Set aside to cool.

Place the bulgur wheat in a bowl, covered with 2cm of tepid water, and leave to sit for 15 minutes.

In the meantime, to create the topping and base, grind all the ingredients, except the bulgur wheat, together in a grinder, high-speed blender or mixer to make a paste. Once you are happy with the consistency, set aside.

Preheat the oven to 190ºC Fan (210ºC/425ºF/Gas 6–7).

Drain the bulgur wheat and squeeze out all the water, as you don't want it to be soft and soggy. Add to the fish mixture and knead together for 5–7 minutes to form a firm but pliable dough that is easy to work with. Split it into two equal-sized pieces and roll each one out into a 30cm circle, using clingfilm on both sides so they don't stick to the work surface; you do not want to use flour on this at all.

Place the first circular piece on the bottom of a deep, round, oiled 30cm dish, and fill it with three-quarters of the potted prawn and onion mix. Spread evenly, then top with the other rolled out half. Press the sides in to secure the filling and use a knife to score the top with some lines for decoration, if desired. Drizzle with olive oil and place in the oven for 25–30 minutes until slightly browned but not too dark.

Stir the remaining potted prawn mixture into the tahini sauce, and serve alongside the *kubbet samak*.

Above: *Gaza Seaport*

Sea bream ceviche with preserved lemons and chilli

سفيتشة سمك بالليمون المخلل والحر

I adore raw, marinated fish, and I think that when you get the sauce right, it just works. Fish is very flexible in terms of accompanying flavours and I wanted to bring some of my favourite ingredients together to make a fresh, tangy and vibrant dish. I really enjoy experimenting and, while I appreciate that this dish is not traditionally Palestinian, it has the essence of the country running through it.

Serves 2–4

400g sushi-grade sea
  bream, thinly sliced
juice of 1 lemon
½ tsp ground coriander
1 red chilli, chopped
50g pomegranate seeds
1 small preserved lemon,
  cut into 1cm chunks
2 sprigs of fresh mint,
  chopped
¼ tsp za'atar
1 tsp salt
2 tbsp olive oil

Combine all the ingredients together and let them sit in the fridge for about 20 minutes so the lemon can begin to cook the fish with its acidity.

Scatter the fish over individual serving plates, making sure you get a little of everything in the serving, and drizzle with some of the liquid marinade. It is light and fresh and tangy. Eat straight away, or store in the fridge until ready to eat.

Seaport at Akka

From left to right: Shatta-grilled prawns with Puy lentil and wild garlic salad; Pomegranate prawns with purslane salad

Pomegranate prawns with purslane salad

قريدس بالرمان مع سلطة البقلة

Prawns are one of my favourite shellfish, and I really love cooking with them. These are sticky and a little sweet too, making them that much better for eating with the tangy purslane salad. This dish is so quick to make and very moreish. It evokes moments by the sea with friends and family – the best way to share a meal.

Serves 4–6

juice of 1 lemon

3 tbsp pomegranate
  molasses

1 tsp salt

2 tbsp olive oil

small bunch of fresh flat-
  leaf parsley, chopped

pinch of chilli flakes

12 medium Arabian Gulf
  prawns, peeled, with
  head and tail attached

For the salad

50g purslane leaves

1 red onion, cut into half-
  moon slices

1 pomegranate, seeded

juice of ½ lemon

2 tbsp apple cider vinegar

1 tsp salt

olive oil, to drizzle

Combine the lemon juice, pomegranate molasses, salt, olive oil, parsley and chilli flakes in a bowl. Add the prawns to the marinade and stir, then leave to marinate for 15 minutes.

Place the prawns into a hot frying pan, reserving the marinade, and cook for 3–4 minutes, turning now and then, until their colour is a pinky orange. They may start to stick or caramelize in the pan, but that is ok. Remove when cooked through and set aside.

Place the remaining marinade into a pan to warm it through slightly.

Combine the purslane leaves, onions and pomegranate seeds in a bowl. Mix together the lemon juice, vinegar and salt to make a dressing. Drizzle the dressing on top of the salad, place the prawns on top of the salad, drizzle with olive oil and the warm marinade and dig in.

Haifa

قريدس مشوي بالشطة مع سلطة عدس وثوم

Shatta-grilled prawns with Puy lentils and wild garlic

Prawns and chillies are a match made in heaven. The flesh of the prawns is sweet and balances so well with the flavour of the chilli. The combination of the chilli paste, wild garlic and lentils with the prawns is earthy, vibrant and fresh. I love adding pulses to prawn dishes as it really makes a meal out of them.

Serves 4–6

1 large onion, diced
50ml olive oil, plus extra to drizzle
6 tbsp red Shatta (page 42), or to taste
350g Puy lentils
2 tsp salt
20–30g wild garlic, roughly chopped or torn
12 large Arabian Gulf prawns (shells removed, but heads and tails intact; this gives more flavour when cooking)
juice of 1 lemon

Place the onions and half the olive oil in a pan and sauté the onions for a few minutes to bring out the flavour. Add 1 large tablespoon of red shatta paste and mix well, then place the lentils and salt into the pan, cover with water by about 5cm, and boil for about 15–20 minutes until the lentils are cooked through.

Drain the liquid, then add the chopped wild garlic and another tablespoon of shatta, stir through the lentils and set aside.

Place the prawns in a pan with the remaining olive oil and cook over a medium heat. Add the remaining shatta and lemon juice and cook for 8–10 minutes, moving the prawns around until they have turned orange. That is when you know they are cooked.

Drizzle with some more olive oil and serve on top of the lentils.

King prawns with carrot and cumin salad

قريدس مع سلطة جزر وكمون

There is a magic that happens when cumin is added to fish. We use cumin quite often at home, and it is a very familiar flavour that we don't shy away from. The spice is mainly found in the carrot salad, as I think these jumbo prawns should not be messed around with too much as they take on such a fabulous and deep flavour when they are charred in the pan. You can leave the shell on or remove it, but definitely keep the heads on as this creates a really flavourful salad; if you close your eyes you really feel as though you are on the coast in Palestine. I love this, and often made it at my deli, always to a great reception. The mint and cumin with the vinaigrette are perfect with this salad.

Serves 3

4 large carrots, grated
1 red onion, cut into rings
bunch of fresh mint leaves
100ml olive oil
50ml white wine vinegar
2 tbsp ground cumin
1 tsp golden caster sugar
1 tsp salt
6 large Arabian Gulf prawns

In a bowl, mix together the carrots, onions and mint. Combine the olive oil, vinegar, cumin, sugar and salt to make a dressing, then pour over the top of the salad. While the sauce is seeping through the carrot mixture, begin your prawns.

Place a large pan on the hob and let it get very hot. You may need to put your extractor fan on for this. Place the prawns into the dry pan and let them begin to char and change colour. This should take about 1–3 minutes on each side, depending on how large your prawns are. I use very large ones as they make this a meal rather than a starter. When they are beginning to secrete their juices slightly and you are happy they have cooked through (they should have turned orange all over), remove them from the pan.

Plate the carrot salad on a large plate, place the prawns on top and serve.

Right: Yaffa coast

Kataifi-wrapped prawns with parsley garlic sauce

قطايف القريدس مع صلصة البقدونس والثوم

When I ran my deli, I used to hold these amazing suppers with up to twenty different dishes on the menu, which were served to share, and which changed every time. I remember working on the menu one day and wondering what I could do with prawns; I was already using some kataifi pastry, and I thought they would be perfect together. I have developed the dish over time, and I think it has reached a really good consistency and flavour, with the sweet prawns, the crunchy pastry and the spicy yogurt dip. The prawns really are the star of the show – they are great as party pieces and very quick to make.

Serves 4–6

16 layers of pulled kataifi pastry with approx. 30 strands in each one
olive oil, for brushing
16 medium prawns, shells removed, but heads and tails intact
sunflower oil, for frying
lemon wedges, to serve

For the sauce
30g fresh flat-leaf parsley
1 garlic clove
juice of ½ lemon
150g Greek yogurt
1 tsp salt

Brush each pastry layer with olive oil and wrap gently around the body of the prawns.

Half-fill a deep pan with sunflower oil and heat to 180ºC. Fry the prawns for about 2–3 minutes until cooked through, then remove and drain for a few minutes on kitchen towel.

Make the sauce by blitzing all the ingredients together in a food processor and serve in a bowl alongside the prawns with a few lemon wedges.

Hills and Orchards

FRUIT AND DESSERTS

Across Palestine you will find areas of uninhabited land that looks like desert, and you will enter other luscious green areas full of fruit trees, such as cherry, fig, lemon and other citrus fruits. You will move on through larger-than-life carob trees, a nearby olive grove, and see nuts and seeds growing. Life is happening in the ground, above the ground and all around you. This is the fabric of Palestine and its people. The trees are tended to like family, and history is cemented in the earth, with the roots growing deeper each year.

The ingredients for our desserts and jams, pickles and preserves, pastries and cakes all come from our hills and orchards. Think of the sweet pastries filled with toasted nuts, the olives that have been picked and pickled by hand – smashed, seasoned and placed in jar after jar – the sauces made from fruit to scatter on the breads made from the fields. What more could you ask for? In Palestine, we literally eat what is grown under our Mediterranean sun, bursting with flavour, and take pride in our produce and our cuisine.

There is history there, a history that has passed from our ancestors, showing us how to use and make the most of what is at our fingertips – and to make it taste fantastic. I remember my mother telling me of my Teta Najla in Yaffa, picking the fruit in the orange and lemon groves, and Teta Huda in Safad, with her mango, apricot and date trees, gathering them up ready to make something delicious. The hills and orchards play a huge role in our life, and as you will see in this chapter, there are many beautiful dishes to be made from them.

Turmusayya, Ramallah

From left to right: Watermelon juice with mint and a dash of orange blossom; Mint and lime juice; Fresh pomegranate and mango juice

Watermelon juice with mint and a dash of orange blossom

بطيخ بالنعنع الحلو مع رشة ماء الزهر

You will never walk past a market stall or vendor in Palestine who is not selling pretty much every kind of fruit and vegetable, and one of our most popular fruits is the watermelon. It is sweet, hydrating and gives you energy during hot days. We make this at home all the time when the weather is warm, and it just takes you back in time. Simple things create such a feeling of nostalgia, and for me that is what this drink represents.

Serves 6

1 watermelon
1 tbsp orange blossom
   water
large bunch of fresh mint
3 tbsp caster sugar
ice cubes

Peel the watermelon and cut the flesh into chunks. I don't bother removing the seeds, as they create a speckled effect that just adds to the end result. Blend the watermelon chunks, or place them in a large bowl and smash them up to release their juices. Add the orange blossom water and three-quarters of the mint, and stir to combine.

Chop the remaining mint until it is really fine, then add it to the sugar in a bowl and set aside.

Once you are happy with the flavour of the drink, add the ice and let it cool down. To serve, place a large ladleful into a glass and scatter the sugared mint on top. This is how my Mama does it. And it's delicious.

Above: *Old City, Al-Quds (Jerusalem)*

Fresh pomegranate and mango juice

عصير رمان ومانجو

There is nothing simple or more satisfying than making fresh juices. Pomegranates are really symbolic of Palestine. You will find juice stands at which people don't operate modern equipment but press with their hands and squeeze the life out of the fruit. Mangoes are also grown in Palestine as we have such a wonderful climate. The combination of the two is simply fantastic. I don't press by hand but use a blender or high-speed mixer to blend the fruit, so I can combine things together as much as I want.

Serves 4–6

seeds of 3 pomegranates
3–4 mangoes, peeled and
   cut into chunks
200g ice cubes
sprig of mint

Put the majority of the pomegranate seeds into your blender, reserving a few to use as a garnish, and blitz. Pour the mix into a bowl and set aside.

Clean the mixer, then add the mangoes and half the ice, and blitz again.

Push the blitzed pomegranate seeds through a sieve to remove all the pulverized bits, and discard them.

Add the sieved pomegranate juice to a jug, along with the iced mango juice and the rest of the ice, and scatter the remaining pomegranate seeds on top and through it. Serve chilled with a sprig of mint.

Mint and lime juice

عصير ليمون اخضر والنعناع

Is there any more perfect combination than mint and lime? For me, this is the ultimate refresher drink and just really wakes you up. I love adding a little bit of mastic to give a flavour of home.

Serves 4–6

large bunch of fresh mint
juice of 20 limes
1 tsp mastic powder
4 tbsp honey
sparkling water
ice cubes

I like to bash the mint in my hands to release the flavour before adding it to the jug. I learnt this from a mixologist in London, so do try it; your hands will smell amazing!

Place the mint and lime juice into a jug with the mastic powder and honey. Top up with sparkling water and add a handful of ice cubes. Mix to combine.

Palestine is famous for its orchards, and the fruits they produce are sublime. My Mama's family loved making jams and here is just a small selection, showcasing the fruits, spices and orange blossom water.

Strawberry, orange blossom and rose jam

فراولة مع ماء الزهر وتطلي الورد

You will need
1 sterilized 750ml jar

750g strawberries
1kg white sugar
juice of ½ lemon
400ml water
2 tsp orange blossom water
5 dried crushed rose buds

Cut the strawberries into quarters, then place in a large pot with the sugar and set aside for a few hours to allow the liquid to seep out of the strawberries naturally and create a lovely flavour.

Add the lemon juice and water, bring to a simmer, and let it cook down for about 30 minutes, then add the orange blossom water and crushed rose buds and stir. Let it cook down for another 5 minutes, then leave to cool, transfer to a sterilized jar and seal until ready to use.

Apple and pistachio jam

تطلي تفاح وفستق حلبي

You will need
1 sterilized 750ml jar

1kg (6–8) Pink Lady or
   Granny Smith apples
650ml water
750g white sugar
1 cinnamon stick
2 cloves
35g pistachios, chopped

Peel the apples and remove most of the core, leaving about 5mm at the base.

Boil the water and sugar together in a pan for 10 minutes, then add the apples, cinnamon and cloves and cook down for about 40 minutes, until the apples are soft and tender and the liquid has thickened and turned golden.

Leave them in the pan overnight, then remove the apples from the jammy sauce and sprinkle a few pistachios into each hole. Return them to the sauce, then transfer everything to a sterilized jar and seal until ready to use.

Yaffa orange jam

تطلي برتقال يافا

You will need
1 sterilized 750ml jar

4 oranges
750g white sugar
450ml water
1 lemon

Peel 2 oranges, removing the pith and keeping thin strands of the peel. Juice these two oranges and place the juice and peel in a pot with the sugar and water.

Cut the remaining oranges into thin slices, with skin on, and then into little pieces. Add to the pan. Remove the lemon peel as well, cut into thin strands, and add to the pan with the juice of half the lemon. Heat gently for 40–50 minutes, until you have a good consistency, then remove from the heat, leave to cool and transfer to a sterilized jar.

From left to right: Apple and pistachio jam; Yaffa orange jam; Strawberry, orange blossom and rose jam

Above: Sataf Village, Al-Quds (Jerusalem)

Mkhalal laymoun

مخلل ليمون

Preserved lemons

I absolutely adore preserved lemons, and in my house we use them a lot, especially with olive and chicken dishes, such as the *Djaj Bil Za'faran Wal Zaytoun* (page 151). Pickling lemons couldn't be easier. And once prepared, they simply need to be left for a few weeks to allow them to become tender in their own juices. You will wonder why you have never made them before, and they taste so much better than shop-bought ones. I think the idea of pickling and preserving really is one of the most important traditions in Palestine. It just creates the most wonderful ingredients for your table. I love having jars of my own pickled vegetables and fruit handy, as I never really know what I'm going to cook each day. The lemons sit proudly next to my pickled beetroot, turnips, cucumbers, olives, and of course my baby aubergines as well. The list of what you can pickle is endless; just be sure to always use sterilized jars to keep your product as fresh and safe as possible.

You will need

1 sterilized 2.5-litre jar

10–12 unwaxed organic
 lemons
150–200g Maldon sea salt

Cut the lemons into quarters lengthways from the top, but stop just before you reach the bottom so you don't cut them all the way through. You want them to still be attached at the end.

Place one lemon in the sterilized jar and press down, adding a tablespoon of salt. Repeat this with the remaining lemons and salt, until you have filled the jar and squeezed the juice out of each lemon. There should be enough juice in the jar to cover the lemons, but if not just squeeze one more to seal them in, then place the lid on the jar. Leave it at room temperature for about 4–5 days, then transfer to the fridge for about 3–4 weeks before using. Trust me, the wait is worth it.

And this is just the base recipe – you could also add some pink peppercorns, a bay leaf or a flavouring of your choice.

Teta Huda's zaytoun

زيتون على طريقة ستى هدى

Pickled olives

If you know anything about Palestine, you will know that we are the land of the olive tree. It is so symbolic for us as it has literally stood the test of time. Many poems were written about this beautiful tree that gives Palestinians not only nutrients but healthcare and skincare products. I use Palestinian olive oil as a moisturizer on my skin and it works wonders. This recipe is so simple, but it helps to have really under-ripe olives, and to watch them mature in your own home, although it does work with ripe ones too.

You will need:

1 x 1.5-litre sterilized jar, and a large stone or meat basher

1kg fresh green olives
1 fresh green chilli, chopped
1 lemon, cut into thin slices
2 garlic cloves, smashed
juice of 1 lemon
olive oil, to cover

Using your stone or basher, smash each olive lightly to create a small crack in it. This will allow the flavours to penetrate during the marinating process.

Place the olives into the sterilized jar, adding the chilli, lemon slices and garlic. Add the lemon juice then fill the jar with olive oil. This oil will not go to waste as you can use it to flavour other things when the olives are gone.

Seal the jar and leave it for a month to get the desired flavour. These can be kept for weeks – we don't really have expiration dates back home!

I like to eat these with some labneh, *makdous*, za'atar and other preserves. It's such a good way to start the day.

Right: *Ramallah*

Opposite (top): Wadi Fukin, Beit Lahem (Bethlehem); *(bottom):* Al-Nasira (Nazareth) market;
This page: Cremisan Valley, Beit Jala

Baklawa

بقلاوة

Pistachio and filo pastry parcels drizzled with sugar syrup

Baklawa is one of the most iconic sweet dishes of the whole of the Levant (though we don't pronounce a 'V' in place of the 'W', as is common). Every country in the region claims this as their own, but I believe it originated in Turkey, where it is recorded that the Sultan used to serve them at a ceremonial procession in the fifteenth century. Wherever it originated, it has travelled widely, through Turkey, Palestine, Syria, Lebanon, Jordan, Greece, Cyprus and beyond – a symbol everyone wants to share.

Serves 10–12

14 sheets of filo pastry (or more if you prefer thicker *baklawa*)

250g butter, melted

250g pistachios, roughly crushed (set some aside for scattering on top)

1 tbsp caster sugar

1 x quantity Sugar Syrup (page 232)

Preheat the oven to 190ºC Fan (210ºC/425ºF/Gas 6–7).

Brush each sheet of filo pastry with melted butter and layer seven sheets on top of each other, then repeat with the other seven sheets, so you have two separate layered piles. Half will be for the base, and the other half for the top. Lay one batch of the filo layers onto a baking sheet to create the base.

Combine most of the pistachios with the sugar and three-quarters of the sugar syrup and scatter all over the pastry base. Place the other seven layers on top and brush with a little more butter. Cut into squares or diamond shapes and place in the oven for about 20 minutes, or until they turn slightly golden.

Remove from the oven and, while hot, drizzle the remaining sugar syrup over the top and leave overnight to soak in. Serve the next day with a scattering of the remaining crushed pistachios.

Warbat bil ishta

وربات بالقشطة

Filo pastries stuffed with sweetened cream

These beauties are one of my favourite desserts; I literally cannot stop eating them once I have started. I adore flaky pastry and sweetened cream cheese, especially when it is homemade. These pastries are enjoyed by all countries in the region, but I think they're most famous in Syria, as this is where I remember eating them. They are perfect to eat during Ramadan to celebrate the end of a long day of fasting, and also great to serve at parties as they really are beautiful.

Makes 18

250g butter
1 x 270g packet of filo
   sheets
1 x quantity Sugar Syrup
   (page 232)
200g slivered pistachios, to
   scatter
dried, crushed rose petals,
   to scatter

For the sweetened cream
2 litres full-fat milk
180ml white wine vinegar
2–3 tbsp caster sugar
1 tbsp butter
150ml double cream

For the sweetened cream, place the milk in a saucepan over a low heat and bring to the boil. Once boiled, add the vinegar. The mixture will split, but that's fine. Pass the milk mixture through a sieve, keeping the curd and discarding all the water.

Add the sugar (according to how sweet you like things) and 1 tablespoon of butter to the curd and mix to combine. Add the double cream, mix well and place in the fridge.

Preheat the oven to 190ºC Fan (210ºC/415ºF/Gas 6–7).

Meanwhile melt the 250g butter and place the filo sheets on a couple of large baking trays. Brush each one with the melted butter, then cut about 18 squares from the pastry. Fold each one in half diagonally and place them in the oven for about 20 minutes until they are golden brown.

When the filo triangles are ready, take them out of the oven, open each one out, stuff them with the sweetened cream and press them back into a triangle shape to hold together.

Drizzle the sugar syrup over the top, scatter over the pistachios and rose petals and serve. Simply wow.

Variation
As an alternative stuffing recipe, cut the crusts off 12 slices of white toasting bread, then use a food processor to blitz them to a chunky powder. Combine with 500ml of double cream and 2–4 tablespoons of golden caster sugar. This stuffing can also be used to fill the *Qatayef* (page 238).

Muntaha's makroutah

Olive oil, fennel seed and date biscuits

These date-filled cookie swirls are to die for. We make them in large batches as they last for up to a week in a sealed container, but trust me they won't make it that long. I love that the pastry is seasoned with fennel and sesame seeds, adding a slight savoury quality to them, which contrasts beautifully with the sweet date paste.

Makes about 25–30 large or 45 smaller biscuits

For the dough
1 tbsp fennel seeds
450g plain flour, plus extra
  for rolling out
150g fine semolina
150ml olive oil
150ml melted butter
1 tsp salt
1½ tbsp milk powder
100g caster sugar
1 x 7g sachet instant yeast
½ tsp baking powder
1 tbsp sesame seeds, plus
  extra for sprinkling

For the date paste
750g pitted Medjool dates,
  chopped
4 tbsp olive oil
2 tbsp melted butter
1 tsp ground cinnamon

Place the fennel seeds into 180ml hot water and leave for 10 minutes to allow the flavours to infuse.

Combine all the ingredients for the dough, along with the drained fennel seeds, together in a bowl. Knead the mixture for about 3–4 minutes, then place in a clean bowl and leave to rise for about 30 minutes.

Preheat the oven to 180°C Fan (200°C/400°F/Gas 6).

Place the chopped dates in a pan with the olive oil, butter and cinnamon and heat gently over a medium–low heat until the dates break down to form a paste, about 10–12 minutes. Once they have broken down, use a spoon and mash them even more, then place on a tray to cool down.

Cut the dough into three or four pieces and roll out onto a floured surface to create rectangles around 1.5cm thick. Or you can cut it into two pieces, which will result in larger biscuits – it's totally up to you.

Once the dough has been rolled, layer the date paste all over it. Ideally, place the date mixture between two layers of clingfilm and use a rolling pin to roll it into a thin layer, the same size as your dough rectangles; this just makes it easier to work with and prevents the dough ripping. Then, using your hands, roll the rectangles from the longest side to form logs. Cut the logs to form biscuits, about 1.5cm thick, and place on a lined baking sheet.

Bake for about 20–30 minutes, depending on the size of your biscuits. You want them to brown slightly on the top, but not too much.

Sprinkle the cooked biscuits with a few sesame seeds, leave to cool, and serve with a cup of hot sage tea.

From left to right: Rose and pistachio éclairs; Pistachio puff swirls

Rose and pistachio éclairs

ايكلير ورد وفستق حلبي

You may be thinking that these are not Palestinian, and you would be right. But if you know me, you know I like to make my own desserts and play with food that brings the essence of home to my kitchen table. So rose and pistachio are definitely up there. These are pretty easy to make and look absolutely delicious. But one word of caution: do not make them too far in advance as they will go soggy. Try to eat them on the day they're made, otherwise you will be disappointed.

Makes 10

85g butter
220ml water
105g plain flour, sifted 3
    times
pinch of salt
3 eggs
100g slivered pistachios,
    to serve
1 tbsp dried, crushed rose
    petals, to serve

For the filling
600ml double cream
3–4 tbsp icing sugar, sifted
1 tbsp rose water
grated zest of 1 lemon

For the icing
225g icing sugar
2 tbsp rose water

Heat the butter and water in a heavy-based pan. Once it has boiled, add the sifted flour and salt and mix vigorously. It will become thick and start to come away from the sides of the pan. Once it has all combined smoothly, remove from the heat and leave to cool on a plate out of the pan. It needs to cool because otherwise the eggs will scramble.

Once the mixture is cool, return to the pan and beat the eggs in one at a time with a wooden spoon, until each egg is fully absorbed and mixed in well. It may seem as though this will never happen, but trust me it will – just keep beating. When you are happy that all the eggs are fully mixed in, transfer the mixture to a piping bag and pipe shapes onto a baking sheet covered with baking parchment. You can make any shapes you like, a traditional eclair, circles – just make sure they will hold a filling.

For the filling, whip the cream with the icing sugar, rose water and lemon zest until thick. Set aside.

Make the icing by simply mixing the ingredients together in a bowl. Set aside.

Preheat the oven to 200ºC Fan (220ºC/425ºF/Gas 7). Place the baking sheet with the eclairs into the oven and bake for 25–30 minutes without opening the door once, otherwise they will collapse. Once they have crisped and browned you will need to skewer them on the base, turn them over and cook for a further 5 minutes so they can dry up inside.

Remove from the oven and leave to cool, then fill them with the cream using a piping bag and the skewered hole, or simply cut them open and fill if you prefer, then drizzle the icing over the top, sprinkle with pistachios and rose petals and serve.

Pistachio puff swirls

فطائر الفستق الحلبي

These beauties are simply an excuse to make a quick and delicious *baklawa* with ready-made puff pastry. I think they are beautiful, and the colour of the pistachios is incredible against the caramelized dough.

Makes 6

2 tbsp caster sugar
1 tbsp water
175g semi-crushed pistachios
320g shop-bought, ready-rolled all-butter puff pastry
1 x quantity Sugar Syrup (page 232), to drizzle
slivered pistachios, to serve

Preheat the oven to 200ºC Fan (220ºC/425ºF/Gas 7).

In a bowl, combine the sugar, water and pistachios.

Place the pre-rolled dough onto a work surface and spread the pistachio mixture over the top.

Roll up the dough along the long edge like a Swiss roll, and cut it into six circles, as though you are making cinnamon buns. Flatten each swirl slightly, then place on a baking sheet and place in the oven for 20–25 minutes until golden brown.

Remove from the oven, drizzle with the sugar syrup while warm, scatter over a few slivered pistachios, and serve.

Ghraybeh biscuits

غريبة

Pistachio biscuits

These delicious shortbread-textured cookies are so reminiscent of my childhood. We used to eat them by the dozen. They are buttery and crumble so quickly in your mouth. I adore making them, especially in the festive season, as they are quick to prepare and hit the spot every time.

Makes 25–30

125g ghee or butter
80g icing sugar
dash of orange blossom
   water
250g plain flour
25–30 pistachios

In a bowl, beat the ghee or butter with the icing sugar until light and fluffy. Add the orange blossom water and mix to combine. Finally, add the flour and incorporate into the mixture until you have a smooth dough. Place in the fridge and leave for an hour.

Preheat the oven to 150ºC Fan/170ºC/325ºF/Gas 3.

Remove the dough from the fridge and knead it gently for 2–3 minutes. Create small walnut-sized balls from the dough and place on a baking sheet. Flatten each ball slightly and add a pistachio to the centre of each one. Cook the biscuits for about 12–15 minutes – you don't want them to turn brown, they should stay a creamy colour.

Remove from the oven and leave to cool. Enjoy them with some sage tea.

Above: *Al-Khalil (Hebron)*

Tamriyeh

تمرية

Semolina strudel

These pastries are simply heaven. They are almost dying out as a dessert, as the pastry is quite tricky to handle, and filling, rolling and frying them seems to be an art that most people are losing. There are very few shops that still serve them, so I had to include this recipe here to give them a revival. It came from my dad's sister Nadia, who loves to bake. The sweetness of the soft centre, with the crunchy strudel-like pastry topped with the dusting of icing sugar is a gorgeous combination.

Makes 8–10

375g plain flour
175–275ml water
sunflower oil, for frying,
    plus extra for shaping the
    dough
icing sugar, to dust

For the filling

220g semolina
300g golden caster sugar
900ml water

Make the dough by putting the flour in a stand mixer with the dough hook fitted and combine with the water – start with 175ml and add more as necessary until the ingredients are fully combined; you want a soft dough that holds itself together in a small ball. Alternatively, bring the dough together using your hands, although this will take slightly longer. Cut the dough into eight balls, lay them out on a well-oiled tray and cover with clingfilm. Leave to rest for 1 hour.

For the filling, place the semolina, sugar and water in a pan over a low heat and keep stirring until it thickens, about 5–6 minutes. You may need to add a little more water. Once it is thick, place it on a baking tray to cool down, and leave in the fridge to set. You need this to be fairly thick and solid as it needs to keep its shape when spooning sections into the delicate pastry. After at least 90 minutes, or preferably overnight, you can begin to use it.

Roll the dough into balls, slightly larger than a golf ball. Then, using your hands and a little sunflower oil, spread each one out very thinly until almost see-through; don't worry too much if it rips as you will be folding it over. When you have a long rectangular shape, take a tablespoon of filling, place it in the centre and fold the long sides over the filling, then fold in the short ends and press to secure the parcels.

Half-fill a deep pan with sunflower oil and heat to 180ºC. Place them in the hot oil and fry until golden and crisp on the outside, flipping once, then remove and drain for a few minutes on some kitchen towel.

Dust some icing sugar on top and eat warm, but not too hot as it will burn your tongue.

Hala's knafeh cheesecake

كعكة كنافة بالجبنة من هالة

This cheesecake is a modern take on the traditional *knafeh* that is known and eaten throughout Palestine. *Knafeh* is the most popular of desserts, and most famous in Nablus. This recipe was given to me by my cousin Hala, and I am so happy that she shared it. The cheesecake mix is mine, but with the added flavours of orange blossom and rose water it is incredible. The kataifi base and topping are simply wonderful and just make you want to eat more. Honestly, you have to try this to see what I'm talking about. You will love it.

Serves 10–12

For the cheesecake mix
2 eggs
300g golden caster sugar
280ml double cream
700g cream cheese (I use
 Philadelphia)
1 tbsp orange blossom
 water
1 tbsp rose water

For the kataifi
600g kataifi pastry
250g butter, melted
1 x quantity Sugar Syrup
 (page 232)

dried, crushed rose petals,
 to serve
50g pistachios, half
 crushed, half left whole,
 to serve

Preheat the oven to 180ºC Fan (200ºC/400ºF/Gas 6). Line a 25cm round loose-bottomed cake tin with baking parchment.

For the cheesecake mix, cream the eggs and sugar in a bowl until doubled in volume and very light in colour.

In a separate bowl, start whipping the cream until it has formed a medium to stiff peak. Fold in the cream cheese, orange blossom water and rose water. Add the egg and sugar mix and beat until well combined and thickened. Set aside while you prepare the base and topping.

For the kataifi, halve the pastry and the butter. Press one batch of pastry into the base of the round cake tin and add one batch of melted butter on top. Bake for 15–20 minutes until the pastry is a golden caramel colour.

Remove the tin from the oven and reduce the oven temperature to 100°C Fan (120°C/230°F/Gas ¼–½). Add half the sugar syrup to the tin while it's still hot, then add the cheesecake mix and bake again for 1 hour.

While this is cooking, shred the second batch of kataifi into a pan over a medium–low heat and toss it with the remaining melted butter. Toast it in the pan until it is golden, then remove from the heat, toss in the remaining sugar syrup and leave to cool completely. Store in a sealed container until ready to use.

Once the cheesecake is cooked, remove from the oven and refrigerate overnight to set.

The next day, add the golden crunchy kataifi pastry on top with the rose petals and pistachios and serve.

Maha's knafeh

كنافة على طريقة مها

Semolina and sweetened cheese bake with lemon sugar syrup

Knafeh is probably the most iconic of Palestinian desserts. It is thought to have originated in Nablus as *knafeh Nabulsiyeh*, but we hear conversations of it coming from Turkey and other countries too, which is common as we all have similar trade routes. There are so many variations of this dessert, but I have chosen one that has a smooth topping. This recipe was given to me by my friends Nadeem and Maya. I met them at a supper club I held with Sami Tamimi and Yotam Ottolenghi, and they raved about how amazing their mother's recipe is; I have to say, they were telling the truth. Thank you, Auntie Maha.

Serves 10

250g ghee
1 x 225g packet of kataifi
    pastry
100g caster sugar
225g coarse semolina flour
30ml rose water
30ml orange blossom
    water
finely chopped pistachios,
    to scatter

For the filling
300g halloumi cheese,
    soaked in water overnight
200g hard mozzarella
    cheese, grated
50g whole milk ricotta
    cheese
2 tbsp each of rose water
    and orange blossom
    water

For the simple syrup
200g caster sugar
240ml water
2 tbsp lemon juice, plus
    1cm piece of peel
1 tbsp each of rose water
    and orange blossom
    water

Preheat the oven to 180ºC Fan (200ºC/400ºF/Gas 6). Use 1 teaspoon of the ghee to grease a 30cm pizza pan. Shred the kataifi pastry in a blender.

Melt the remaining ghee in a pan and add the sugar. Add the pastry and combine by hand over a very low heat. Add the semolina flour and mix with the shredded pastry. Slowly add the rose water and orange blossom water, kneading until it sticks together well. This should be done over the lowest heat possible.

Press the dough into the greased pizza pan to about a 3mm thickness (or to your desired thickness). Put the dough in the oven for 15–20 minutes, but watch it very carefully as it can burn. It should become a light golden brown on top.

While the dough is baking, drain and rinse the halloumi cheese. Mix all the cheeses together by hand in a bowl. Add the rose water and orange blossom water and incorporate, then set aside.

For the simple syrup, combine the sugar and water in a small saucepan and bring to the boil. Add the lemon juice and the piece of lemon peel and leave to simmer for about 5 minutes. Remove from the heat, add the rose water and orange blossom water and leave to cool.

When the dough is ready, remove it from the oven and leave to cool for about 10 minutes. Spread the cheese evenly over the top. Return to the oven for about 2 minutes until the cheese slightly melts and evens out. Remove from the oven and leave to cool for another 10 minutes.

Shake gently until it detaches from the pan, then carefully flip it on to a serving dish, drizzle with a thin layer of cooled simple syrup and scatter over the chopped pistachios.

Pistachio, courgette and lemon cake

كعكة كوسا وليمون والفستق الحلبي

I started making this cake years ago, when I was running my deli. I really prefer it to carrot cake, and the green of the pistachio slivers running through it make it not only beautiful but delicious. It is lighter because it has an olive oil base which keeps it fluffy and moist, rather than a more crumbly butter base. The pistachios must be good quality, so please do make sure you use the best you can find.

Serves 6–8

250ml olive oil

4 eggs

225g golden caster sugar

225g plain flour

1 heaped tsp baking
   powder

½ tsp bicarbonate of soda

½ tsp salt

1 tsp ground ginger

180g courgettes, grated

150g pistachios, chopped

For the icing

150g icing sugar

juice of 1 lemon

Preheat the oven to 180ºC Fan (200ºC/400ºF/Gas 6). Line a 20cm cake tin with baking parchment.

In a large bowl, mix together the olive oil, eggs and sugar.

Sift the flour, baking powder, bicarbonate of soda, salt and ginger into a separate bowl, then add to the sugar and eggs and stir to combine. Now add the courgettes and pistachios and stir through, then transfer the mixture to the tin.

Place the cake in the oven for about 50–60 minutes until a skewer inserted into the centre comes out clean. Leave the cake to cool for a few minutes in the tin, then transfer to a wire rack to cool completely.

For the icing, mix the icing sugar and lemon juice together to create a smooth texture, then pour over the cooled cake. Serve in lovely thick slices.

Right: *Al Quds (Jerusalem)*

Auntie Samira's qizha

Auntie Samira's qizha

قزحة من خالتي سميرة

Black sesame cake

Qizha is another dessert that is disappearing off the local stalls in Palestine. This beautiful charcoal-coloured cake includes nigella seeds (*habbet il barakah*), which translates as 'the seeds of blessing'. The Prophet Mohammad (peace be upon him) said that these seeds can cure anything except death, and they are still used to cure many ailments to this day. I personally use the oil to treat and heal my own skin, and it works for me – imagine the good it does to you on the inside when you eat it.

Serves 10–12

300g plain flour
130g semolina
130g caster sugar
220ml warm water
1 x 7g sachet instant yeast
1 tsp sesame seeds
180ml olive oil
130g nigella sativa seeds
raw soaked almonds, to
   decorate

For the sugar syrup
400g caster sugar
250ml water

Line a 20cm cake tin with baking parchment.

Combine the flour, semolina, sugar, water, yeast and sesame seeds together in a bowl, by hand or using a stand mixer.

Blend the olive oil and nigella seeds together in a blender to create a black oily paste. Add this to the flour mix and stir in.

Make sure the mixture is well combined, then place it in your lined tin and flatten it down. Take a knife and create a shape on top of the cake, pushing all the way down to the bottom. This is necessary as when it cooks the syrup needs to get right into the grooves.

Place the almonds around the top of the cake, inside the marked segments. This will help indicate when the cake has cooked too, as the almonds will brown, then let it sit for about 30 minutes in a warm place.

Preheat the oven to 180ºC Fan (200ºC/400ºF/Gas 6). When ready, place the cake on the middle shelf of the oven for about 35–40 minutes.

While it is cooking, heat the sugar and water in a pan and let them cook down to create a nice syrup. This should take about 10–12 minutes. Set aside.

When the cake is ready and still hot, drizzle all of the syrup over the top and let it sit for about 30 minutes before serving to allow the sugar syrup to soak in. Nigella seeds are quite bitter, so the sugar syrup is very important in this dessert.

Chocolate and labneh cake with slivered pistachios

كعكة شوكولاتة ولبنة بالفستق الحلبي

This cake came about by accident and I just had to include it here. I was running a cooking class and forgot to buy soured cream, so decided instead to use the labneh in my fridge as a substitute. I was panicking and worrying about it going wrong, but it actually worked perfectly – even better than I thought it would – and I have never stopped making it this way. Sometimes the best things come to you when everything is upside down, and this was one of those occasions. If you don't have labneh, you can use extra thick Greek yogurt.

Serves 8

4 eggs, beaten
110g soft butter
110g golden caster sugar
110g soft light brown sugar
5 tbsp labneh
1 tsp vanilla extract
170g plain flour
55g cocoa powder
pinch of salt
1½ tsp bicarbonate of soda
1 tsp baking powder
handful of slivered
  pistachios (about 70g)

For the icing
170g unsalted softened
  butter
200g icing sugar
170g labneh
70g cocoa powder, sifted
2 tsp vanilla paste

Preheat the oven to 180°C Fan (200°C/400°F/Gas 6). Line a 900g loaf tin with baking parchment.

In a bowl, mix together the eggs, butter, sugars and labneh, then add the vanilla extract. Beat for a couple of minutes.

Sift the flour and cocoa powder into a separate bowl, then add the salt, bicarbonate of soda and baking powder. Add this to the egg and sugar mixture and mix for about 30–60 seconds.

Place in the tin and cook for about 45 minutes until a skewer inserted into the centre comes out clean. Leave the cake to cool for a few minutes in the tin, then transfer to a wire rack to cool completely.

For the icing, combine the butter and icing sugar together in a bowl and mix well. Add the labneh, sifted cocoa powder and vanilla paste and mix for about 2 minutes until the icing is smooth and creamy. Place in the fridge to firm up slightly.

When the icing is ready and the cake is cooled, spread the icing over the cake, scattering the chopped pistachios on top.

Hilbeh

حلبة

Fenugreek cake

Hilbeh is made using fenugreek seeds that have been soaked in water overnight then mixed with an array of other seeds that are just so good for you. The combination of all of them is simply wonderful. Traditionally, this is made much thinner than I have done it here, but I just prefer it thicker. You can use the same recipe but make it in a large tray to thin it out. This cake has a very distinct flavour and is used as a digestive aid, so it not only tastes good but is good for you too.

Makes 20–24

2 tbsp fenugreek seeds, soaked overnight in water (refresh the water a couple of times to remove any bitterness)
250g medium coarse semolina
50g plain flour
50ml olive oil
50ml melted butter
2 tbsp milk powder
80ml warm water
1 x 7g sachet instant yeast
½ tsp baking powder
1 tbsp caster sugar
1 tsp salt
1 tsp sesame seeds
1 tsp nigella sativa seeds
2 tbsp tahini
20–24 raw soaked almonds
1 x quantity Sugar Syrup (page 232), to drizzle

Drain the soaked fenugreek seeds – they should have swollen in size, which is what we're looking for. Combine the drained seeds in a large bowl with all the remaining ingredients, except the tahini, almonds and sugar syrup.

Place the tahini on the base of a 23 x 32cm cake tin and add the mixture over the top. Cover with a tea towel and leave in a warm place for 30 minutes to rise slightly.

Preheat the oven to 190ºC Fan (210ºC/415ºF/Gas 6–7). Cut the cake mixture into diagonal shapes and place one almond in the centre of each shape. Bake in the oven for 30–35 minutes, until golden.

Once cooked, take it out of the oven and drizzle generously with the sugar syrup. Leave for 45 minutes so the syrup can soak through, then serve.

Right: *Downtown Ramallah*

Qatayef

قطايف

Soft pancakes filled with cream in an orange blossom sugar syrup

Qatayef are soft, pillowy pancakes that are simply gorgeous. They are freshly made and stuffed with all sorts of fillings – cream, pistachios, walnuts, cheeses . . . They are sometimes eaten soft and sometimes fried, the choice is yours – the method of preparing them and putting them together is the same.

I love making these for special occasions such as Eid and birthdays, as they are such a treat and also look beautiful. Their texture is so unctuous that you just want to eat more than one. Every family has their own way of making them, and this is the way we do it at home.

Makes 25–30

For the pancakes
500ml warm milk
500ml warm water
1 x 7g sachet instant yeast
½ tsp baking powder
¼ tsp salt
3 tbsp caster sugar
300g plain flour
170g fine semolina

1 x quantity Sweetened Cream or variation (page 212)
sunflower oil, for deep-frying (optional)
1 x quantity Sugar Syrup (page 232), mixed with 2 tsp orange blossom water
crushed pistachios, to scatter
dried, crushed rose petals, to scatter

Combine all the pancake ingredients in a bowl, then set aside for 30 minutes to allow to rise.

When the mixture has rested and the gluten has grown, place a pan on the hob over a low heat and grease it with a little oil. Place a small ladleful of the mixture into the pan and let it cook. You should start to see small air bubbles on the top. When it is golden on the bottom and cooked through, with bubbles visible on top, remove from the pan, set aside and repeat with the remaining mixture.

Once you have made all of them, you can start stuffing them. I am using the sweetened cream filling from the *Warbat Bil Ishta* (page 212), but feel free to add your own chosen filling. Place a dollop of stuffing in the centre of one pancake. If you are serving straight away, begin pressing the edges of the pancake together on one side, but stop halfway, so you have a semicircle that is open on one side, exposing some of the filling. Repeat with the rest.

If you are deep-frying, seal the pancakes all the way. Half-fill a deep pan with oil, heat it to 180ºC, and fry the pancakes until slightly golden and a little crisp. Remove from the oil and drain on kitchen towel for a few minutes.

To serve either version, drizzle with the orange blossom sugar syrup, scatter over the pistachios and rose petals and serve.

Maftoul bil sukar

مفتول بالسكر

Palestinian couscous with sugar and butter

When we were little, my Mama would literally run around like a headless chicken at home – especially when all five of us had a friend over too. Our house was chaotic to say the least, but it was always fun. She would whip us up the most delicious treats, and this was one of my favourites, and also my friends' too, as it was unusual for them and they had never eaten it before. Maftoul is a Palestinian couscous used mainly in savoury dishes, but here it is sugared, buttered and divine. It takes about 10 minutes to make, depending on the type of maftoul: some are tiny and some are large, so please use your own judgement. My Mama used to eat this with her mama, and so the tradition continues.

Serves 2–4

150g dried maftoul
2 tbsp golden caster
   sugar, plus extra to serve
   (optional)
40g butter
dried, crushed rose petals,
   to scatter

Place the maftoul in a deep pan with the sugar, and add enough water to cover by a couple of centimetres. Bring to the boil to cook through the maftoul; depending on its size, this should take about 10–12 minutes. Drain the remaining water, add the butter and stir over the heat for a minute or two.

Place the maftoul into a bowl and scatter over some more sugar, if desired. Scatter with the rose petals, serve and eat straight away.

Above: Marj Ibn Amer Plain, Jenin

Manfousheh (halawet il tahineh) منفوشة (حلاوة الطحينة)

Tahini halva

Halawet il tahineh is such a symbol of the Middle East. It is a sweet that I have eaten ever since I was a child, and it was always present on the table after dinner or just sitting around the house for anyone who wanted to pick some up for a quick snack. This recipe is incredibly easy, and if you like tahini, then this is the recipe for you.

It's incredible how such a small number of ingredients can make something so delicious, and I always wonder at how such things came about and who thought of them. Whenever I eat these, I remember my aunties sitting together, laughing, chatting, drinking tea and nibbling at them in our house, whiling away the hours. Memories and food have such a strong bond for me, and I think this is why I cook – to remember and highlight moments of my life that have truly brought me joy.

Makes 8–10 slices

200g icing sugar
150g dried milk powder
280g tahini
70g pistachios

Place the icing sugar and milk powder into a bowl and mix together. Add the tahini and stir through. It should come together to form a fairly crumbly 'dough'. If it is too wet, add more icing sugar or milk powder. You want this to be firm but still pliable.

Line a 900g loaf tin with clingfilm and place all the pistachios on the bottom, then add the mixture over the top, cover with clingfilm and leave to set in the fridge. I leave it overnight so it gets really firm. Turn it out onto a plate and serve in slices with some coffee.

Above: *Sir Village, Jenin.*

Karawya

كراوية

Sweetened caraway pudding

Karawya is a dessert that is usually made to celebrate a birth, as it is thought that it helps provide a lactating mother with the nutrients she needs during this time. It is filled with caraway and cinnamon and decorated with plenty of soaked nuts, such as almonds and pistachios. This dish only takes a short time to put together, but it does need to set in the fridge for a few hours. Alternatively, you could serve it warm, if you prefer; at my house we only eat it cold.

Serves 12–14

150g rice flour

1.15 litres water

170–200g golden caster sugar (use more or less depending on how sweet you like things)

3 heaped tbsp ground caraway

3 heaped tbsp ground cinnamon

100g almonds

100g pistachios

100g walnuts

100g pine nuts

100g dried, crushed rose petals

5 tsp ground pistachios

5 tsp shredded coconut

Put the flour, water, sugar, caraway and cinnamon into a pan over a medium heat and whisk. You will need to keep whisking so it doesn't stick and burn. You are looking for a nice thick consistency.

Once you have reached the desired thickness, about 10–12 minutes, remove from the heat and place either in one large high-edged serving dish or divide it between small wide-rimmed glasses, and place in the fridge for a minimum of 2 hours to set completely.

Soak all the whole nuts separately in water for 1 hour to allow them to swell up.

Once you are ready to serve, dress the dessert with the almonds, pistachios, walnuts, pine nuts and rose petals, and scatter the ground pistachios and shredded coconut over the top.

Um Ali

ام علي

Middle Eastern brioche bread and butter pudding

This delicious dessert is the Middle Eastern equivalent of bread and butter pudding. For me, this is on another level – the flavours and essence of the Middle East run through it, with the nutmeg, cinnamon and orange blossom. There are a few stories of where the name originates, and one is of Um Ali (the mother of Ali), the first wife of Sultan Ezz El Din Aybek, whose reign began in 1250. When the Sultan died, it was expected that the throne would go to the first son of the first wife, Ali. However, the Sultan's second wife also wanted her son to be the Sultan. Um Ali was not willing to leave the throne to anyone other than her first born, so she decided to eliminate the threat. She succeeded and her son Ali became Sultan. Um Ali then made this dessert to celebrate his victory. This is not a traditional Palestinian dessert – its origins are in Egypt – but as with so many other dishes from in and around the area, food travelled in the same way as people and stories.

Serves 8–10

350g brioche bread, cut
   into 2.5cm cubes
300g firm apples, peeled,
   cored and cut into chunks
135g caster sugar
squeeze of ½ lemon
150g golden sultanas
1 tbsp vanilla bean paste
1 tbsp ground cinnamon
½ tsp grated nutmeg
small pinch of ground
   cardamom powder
¼ tsp ground cloves
grated zest of 1 orange
1 tbsp orange blossom
   water
500ml milk
4 eggs, whisked
handful of slivered
   pistachios, to serve
handful of almonds, to
   serve

Place the bread and apples in a 30cm baking dish or cake tin with the sugar and lemon juice and mix to combine. Add the sultanas on top.

In a large bowl, combine all the remaining dry ingredients, except the nuts, with the milk and eggs and pour over the bread mixture, making sure the apples and bread are well covered. Leave in the fridge for an hour or so.

Preheat the oven to 180ºC Fan (200ºC/400ºF/Gas 6). Cover the dish or tin with foil and cook for 20 minutes, then remove the foil and cook for a further 30 minutes until golden on top.

Remove from the oven, scatter with the nuts and serve.

From left to right: Bouza bil tahineh wal simsim;
Bouza bil ishta wal fustoq

Bouza bil ishta wal fustoq

بوظة القشطة بالفستق الحلبي

Palestinian ishta ice cream with pistachios

When we were younger this was all we wanted to eat. All day, every day. I remember when we used to visit my grandmother, she would take us to the market stalls and buy this for us, but it was always better when she made it herself, because it meant that we could learn too. And who wouldn't want to know how to make this? It is such a delicious ice cream that it takes me back to our time with her in Syria. This is most famous in Ramallah, in a place called Rukab, which is the ultimate destination in which to try this ice cream – it is so worth it.

Serves 10–12

700ml full-fat milk
3 tbsp cornflour
225g caster sugar
460ml double cream
2 tbsp orange blossom
    water
1 tsp crushed mastic
200g pistachios

Combine all the ingredients, except the pistachios, in a large pan and bring to the boil. Reduce the heat to a simmer and keep stirring with a whisk until the mixture thickens. This should take about 10–12 minutes.

Once it is ready, place in a bowl and leave to cool down in the fridge for a couple of hours. Then place in a freezerproof container and transfer to the freezer.

After about 4 hours, remove it from the freezer and mix to prevent any ice crystals forming, then return to the freezer. Repeat after another 4 hours, but this time spread the ice cream onto a flat tray, cover with clingfilm and return to the freezer overnight.

The following day, crush most of the pistachios and scatter them generously over the ice cream. Remove the ice cream from the tray and begin rolling it like a roulade. Once it is rolled, take the rest of the pistachios and roll the roulade over them to cover the outside of the ice cream. Return to the freezer and, when ready, after about 1 hour, slice into lovely rings and serve.

Bouza bil tahineh wal simsim

بوظة بالطحينة والسمسم

Tahini ice cream with sesame seeds

We use tahini in everything – well I do anyway. In *Palestine on a Plate* I made tahini brownies, which I have been making for years as I don't eat peanuts, and they are so delicious and moreish. The Palestinian ice cream opposite is so traditional and takes me back to my childhood every time, but this one is new for me, ever since I thought how wonderful it would be to have an ice cream with tahini as the base. It is literally a little piece of home, and it's good.

Serves 10

1 litre full-fat milk
500ml double cream
1 vanilla pod, scraped
6 egg yolks
300g golden caster sugar
350g tahini
sesame seeds, to scatter

Scald the milk and double cream in a pan with the vanilla pod and seeds. Once it has come to the boil, let it simmer for 5 minutes over a very low heat.

Set the pan aside for 5–10 minutes while you cream together the egg yolks and sugar in a bowl until light and fluffy. Stir through the tahini, then add the warm milk slowly to this mixture and mix well to combine everything together. You don't want the milk to be too hot otherwise it will scramble the eggs.

When you have reached a good, smooth consistency, transfer to a pan and heat gently until it thickens slightly, about 6–7 minutes, then leave it to cool down.

Place in a container or an ice cream machine and churn. If you're not using a machine, place in the freezer and leave for a few hours, then mix; repeat this two or three times, every couple of hours, to prevent it from crystallizing. It should be creamy and smooth. Scatter with sesame seeds and serve.

@PICTUREPERFE

Opposite, clockwise from top left: *Old City, Al-Quds (Jerusalem);*
Surda, Ramallah and Al-Bireh; Battir, Beit Lahem (Bethlehem);
Ramallah; **This page:** *Sabastia, Nablus; Old City, Nablus; Gaza*

INDEX

CREDITS

Location images: Ahmed Alomary: pages 2–3, 9 (b), 14–15, 25, 36, 38, 52–53, 58, 79, 85 (b), 88, 98, 104, 111 (t), 133, 136–137, 188, 210, 240, 243; Petra Costandi: page 33, 63; Dina Dahmash: pages 4, 6 (tl), 8 (bl), 16 (t), 17, 54 (br), 252 (tl), 253 (br); Fiona Dunlop: pages 12 (b), 70; Elias Halabi: pages 8 (tl, tr), 13 (bl), 26, 54 (t, bl), 71, 85 (t), 108–109, 110, 111 (b), 142, 184–185, 252 (br), 253 (t); Nayef Hammouri: pages 6 (bl), 13 (br), 124, 222; Ghassan Hussein: page 194; Joudie Kalla: page 220; Safaa Khateeb: pages 6 (br), 8 (cl); Fadi Khirieh: page 252 (bl, tr); Wissam Nassar: Pages 6 (tr), 13 (t), 44–45, 158–159, 160–161, 166, 178, 182, 253 (bl); Nicki Pennington: pages 82–83, 208; Samer Sharif: pages 9 (tl); Natalie Tahhan: pages 9 (tr), 43, 55, 68, 75, 114, 152, 154, 165, 172, 174, 190, 205, 209, 228, 236, 244, 251; Jumanah Tubaileh: pages 8 (br), 12 (tl, tr), 37, 49, 189, 198

(b *bottom*; t *top*; c *centre*; l *left*; r *right*)

Author image (page 256): Stuart Ovenden

We would also like to thank Habibi interiors for their backgrounds, and Ceramica Blue for their plates and platters.

Acknowledgements

Firstly, I would like to thank my Mama Fadia and Baba Fathi. Without all your support and love, none of this would have happened. Palestine would not exist for us without you and your stories. The lessons we have learnt of our rich history made this book so easy to put together. How else could I have portrayed Palestine, other than through your eyes and memories, and the memories passed down from your own parents. Thank you for loving her and teaching us about her, and for making Palestine a part of us.

Jacqui, how pleased was I to have a go at writing my second book with you. It has been a pleasure to work with you and I will never forget you. Thank you for loving Palestine and all her culinary delights.

Heather, it's so great to be a part of your team and to work with you to make not only my first book a reality, but this book also. Thank you for being there and for making this happen from day one!

Michel, what a pleasure to share, love and live Palestine with you in creating these books. I hope you are proud, as I am, to be working with you.

Rachel C, working with you and Jamie so closely was a breeze. We had the same ideas and this shows beautifully in the end result. What a lovely team to create such a fabulous book. Rachel M, how very patient you are with all my edits. I have to say that I am always so nervous of this part, but you make it seem like a breeze.

Lucy, yet again your styling has been on point and really captures everything Palestine is about. The pictures would never have worked without you.

To my sisters, brother, and friends, what a year! You have all been the most wonderful support creating this book with me, listening to me and going through each chapter with me. You really are amazing and are all a part of the book. Your opinions were impactful and kept me focused and it shows in every little detail. I love you all.

Mariam, Suma and Fatimah, thank you for all your help, and for prepping with me for this book. It really is so wonderful to have you as a part of this. And all your efforts show with the perfect little details in the book.

Rex, look at how gorgeous the fish section is. It couldn't have been more beautiful with all your fresh, gorgeous products. You are a star! J. Baker and Andreas, thank you for always supplying me with such fabulous groceries that really make the food stand out and taste so fabulous. Samir, my butcher, your produce has played a pivotal role in this book, as it is such a huge part of our dinner table, and it could not be more fabulous. I'm so happy to have found you!

Special thanks to my favourite food tasters, Rana and Meera, all my supperclub guests, and my clients for the last 15 years. This doesn't happen without you. You are the reason that Palestine is alive and kicking!

With love always, Joudie

About the author

Joudie Kalla has been a chef for over 20 years. She trained at Leith's School of Food and Wine, and worked in many prestigious restaurants before going on to run her own successful catering business. She opened a Palestinian deli, Baity Kitchen, in Chelsea, from 2010–2013 to much acclaim, before turning her sights to writing her first bestselling cookbook *Palestine on a Plate*. She runs cookery courses, catering events and supperclubs, as well as consulting on food projects. If you want to keep in touch and see her daily creations, follow her on Instagram @palestineonaplate